To Margaret
for her support
and
to the Afghan cameleers and their camels
for their effort

Published in Australia by ABC Books for the
AUSTRALIAN BROADCASTING CORPORATION
GPO Box 9994 Sydney NSW 2001

First published in hardback in 2005
Reprinted May 2006
First published in paperback in 2006

National Library of Australia Cataloguing-in-Publication
Brian, Janeen, 1948–. Hoosh! Camels in Australia.
Bibliography. Includes index. For children aged 9+
ISBN 0 7333 1504 6 (hardback)
ISBN 0 7333 1388 4 (paperback)
1. Camels - Australia - Juvenile literature.
I. Australian Broadcasting Corporation. II. Title.
636.295

Edited, designed and typeset by Margaret Hamilton
Cover design by Christabella Designs
Front cover photograph: Getty Images
Set in Times Roman and Optima
Diagram of camel skeleton on p11 by Lorenzo Lucia
Maps by Laurie Whiddon
Colour reproduction by Colorwize, Adelaide
Printed and bound in Malaysia by Tien Wah Press

2 4 5 3

HOOSH!

Camels in Australia

Janeen Brian

ABC
Books

CONTENTS

At first they are queer, awkward, slow, hard to understand, stupid, smelly, unapproachable and unfriendly, horribly noisy with their awful groans at loading time, generally repulsive, and trying on the nerves of everyone in a hurry. Their pack-saddles always seem to be wretched affairs, continually coming to pieces and the whole process of travelling by camel seems antiquated and exasperated.

But when the temperature begins to pass 100°F day after day, when the feed disappears and only dry brambles can be found, and finally, when water and the possibility of water becoming nothing but a wild hope, then the camel comes into his own.

There he kneels, uncomplaining and unconcerned, a tower of strength and comfort, living on the fat of his hump and good for another 200 miles.

C.T. Madigan, explorer of the Simpson Desert, 1939.

Unlike other animals introduced to Australia, camels helped the new settlers. Along with their hard-working Afghan handlers, they criss-crossed the semi-arid regions and hot, dry deserts, carting and carrying as beasts of burden.

Desert winds may have blown away the camels' tracks, but their footsteps were the life-blood for those pioneers who lived and worked in the isolated outback. Camels brought food supplies and water, material for housing, machinery, education and communication. Their endurance made it possible for expeditions and survey work to be carried out, for roads and railways to be built, for mines to be developed and for wool and wheat to be exported. Camels also meant rides to picnics, mail deliveries, medical visits and races.

The camel and its handler were as important to the history of the outback as the bullockies and horse teamsters. And where the camel trod, others followed.

Writing this book has been a wonderful adventure! A publisher suggested the idea to me over six years ago. I began to research in libraries, on the internet and in museums, until I had an envelope of photos and a folder full of information. The book did not eventuate, but the idea came up again in 2003. Ten months, or 1,500 hours of researching and writing later, I had 36 folders bulging with information, emails, photo ideas, interview transcriptions, newspaper cuttings, film notes and four plastic folders containing approximately 300 photos.

As part of my research, I travelled the outback. I watched the Voyages Camel Cup in Alice Springs, where camels strode, necks stretched, at full gallop around a racetrack. I interviewed people involved with camel farms and the tourist industry, as well as others involved in businesses, including the exportation of camels. I've even ridden a camel and tasted camel milk!

As much as I wanted Australian children and adults to discover what wonderful creatures camels are, I also wanted them to understand the enormous part camels played in the lives of explorers, pioneers and settlers — and consequently the development of the interior. The value of camels can never be really appreciated until you experience those long, hot stretches of outback Australia and see the vastness of the country, or walk about isolated homesteads or townships now in ruins.

I sincerely acknowledge the Afghan cameleers and their vital contribution to the lives of Australians. And I acknowledge the camel who, to me, typifies the uniqueness of the Australian outback; a charismatic survivor.

Today the Australian camel thrives in desolate outback regions. But what is its future?

Janeen Brian

IMAGINE A CAMEL

THE ORIGINS OF THE CAMEL

Imagine a camel the size of a large rabbit! About 40 million years ago, a small, fine-boned animal with a short neck and no hump lived in North America. It was the first true member of the Camelidae family and the ancestor of today's camel.

Over thousands of years, those creatures evolved into gazelle- and giraffe-like animals. They also adapted to dry areas. However, the spread of North American grasslands greatly reduced much of these animals' natural vegetation and only the smaller of the species and the very large, leaf-browsing animals survived.

About three million years ago, when the sea level lowered, a bridge on the sea floor between Alaska and Siberia, called the Bering Strait, was exposed. The larger camels migrated over this temporary stretch of dry land and moved into Asia. Later they continued into Eastern Europe, the Middle East and North Africa.

The smaller camels went south into South America. Those migrations saved the camel species, for none exists in North America today.

Two types of camel developed from these larger animals, and they are the ones we see today: the one-humped camel and the two-humped camel. No-one is certain when the humps developed. It's a possibility they grew after the animals were domesticated, or tamed, by humans.

The camels that settled in the mountainous desert country of Central Asia were faced with severe climate changes: bitter, fierce winters with temperatures, as low as – 40°C, and hot summers of 55°C.

TWO HUMPS

Bactrian camels, or mountain camels, are two-humped. They are tough and hardy with short legs and stout feet to navigate rocky slopes, slippery ice and snow. Their long, thick winter hair resembles large, shaggy overcoats.

Centuries ago, Bactrian camels and their handlers travelled back and forth across a wild, bleak and dangerous stretch of Central Asia. The route linked China, Central Asia, Persia, Western Asia and Europe. It was named the 'Silk Road', because of the Chinese silk cloth that the camels carried. They also carried other exotic luxury goods, like porcelain china, gold and unusual animals. Europeans in the West were prepared to pay dearly for these highly-prized goods.

Bering Strait made it possible for camels to migrate from America to Asia and subsequently survive.

A Bactrian camel and calf. The name 'Bactrian' came from a place called Baktria, in Afghanistan.

Nowadays, most Bactrians are domesticated and live in Mongolia, China, India, Pakistan, Afghanistan, Kazakhstan and Uzbekistan. A small population of wild Bactrians lives in the Gobi Desert and is listed as critically endangered.

> Llamas are closely related to camels. A camel-cross-Llama was born in Dubai in the United Arab Emirates, in 1997. It was named Rama the Cama!

ONE HUMP

The one-humped camel is called an Arabian, but is now more commonly called a dromedary camel, from the Greek word *dromos,* meaning *street* or *running*. It migrated into the arid regions of the Middle East, Northern India and Africa, especially the Sahara Desert. Dromedaries endure hot desert life, where vegetation and water are scarce. Because of its habitat, it's also called the plains camel.

A Bactrian camel and an Arabian camel can mate — as they're from the same animal family. But the result isn't a camel with three humps! Instead, the back area 'becomes one big hump and the camel generally looks big and overweight', says a camel handler from Queensland. Few of these crossbreeds are found in Australia.

It's thought that camels were the earliest animals domesticated by humans. They are true beasts of burden. They carry passengers and goods. But they can also be harnessed to pull wheeled vehicles, ploughs or waterwheels. Desert-dwelling nomads travel constantly in search of food or water for themselves or their animals. They value their camels because the animals give them meat, milk, dung fuel, leather and wool for making mats, blankets and clothing.

Camel festivals or fairs are held regularly, particularly in desert and semi-desert areas where camels are considered the prime work animals. The fairs are great occasions where people come from far and wide to trade camels and take part in the festivities. There's an air of excitement as open, dusty plains fill with hundreds of camel owners making camp alongside their animals. Tents spring up, full of items for sale: camel nose-pegs, bells, hobbles and brightly embroidered saddles. Events include camel parades, races, acrobatics and camel-fur cutting competitions.

Today, four members of the camel family live in South America: domesticated Llamas (above and below) and alpacas. Guanacos and vicunas live in the wild.

More than a hundred years ago, shiploads of dromedaries were imported from India and Pakistan to work in the arid regions of Australia. Their descendents form the large population of feral camels here today.

DROMEDARIES IN AUSTRALIA

A camel may look gangly and lumpy, with its head in the air and a snooty expression on its face, but it's about as perfect a desert design as you could find.

It's a large, tough, smelly animal, tall as a doorway, with an average weight of 450 kilograms. It can go where wheeled trucks and cars can't. It can carry heavy loads. And it can survive in dry, waterless areas where other animals would perish.

Between 500,000 and 700,000 feral camels live in Australia today. These dromedaries are descendents of the camels imported from India and Pakistan in the nineteenth century. Their habitats include eucalypt forest, mallee, acacia woodland, desert heathlands, and the saltbush and bluebush areas that edge crusty salt lakes. Most herds are found in Western Australia and in the centre of the continent.

These dromedaries walk across burning gibber plains, treeless landscapes and steep sand-dunes. They're faced with wild dust storms, hot desert days and bone-cold nights. The search for water is never-ending.

SURVIVAL

A camel survives because of its remarkable adaptations to desert life. To stay alive, the camel must keep cool and conserve water in every possible way. Each part of the animal is like a small miracle.

BODY

Legs

A camel has four long, strong legs and a ropey tail about 50 centimetres long. Air circulates around the animal's legs, helping to keep it cool. With its powerful upper leg muscles it can walk all day in search of food, and support loads of up to 450 kilograms or more — the weight of an average-sized camel.

The worn, leathery patches on the camel's leg joints and chest look as if the fur has been rubbed off. But

Camels prefer to feed on juicy, salty plants, leaves of trees and shrubs and also herbs, rather than grass.

those calloused areas are natural and already visible on baby camels a few months old. They protect the skin and muscles from damage when the camel kneels or lies on hot or rough ground.

Feet

The foot consists of two toes. Connecting them is a thick, heat-resistant, cushioned pad that spreads as the camel puts its foot down. Acting like a broad snowshoe, it prevents the animal from sinking into light soil or sand. Like cows, horses and other ungulates (animals with hoofs), the camel also has hoofs, but it doesn't walk on them. They sit like small toenails at the end of each foot. As a camel walks, it makes almost no sound. Nor do its feet cut into the surface of the soil and cause it to erode.

Camels become nervous about slipping in mud as their feet are unstable. Any stumble or heavy fall could cause a broken leg, hip or breastbone. Severe falls may mean death.

A working camel usually travels about 32 – 40 kilometres each day, at a speed of around 3–5 kilometres per hour. Camels prefer to walk, especially on a hot day, but can gallop or pace when there's a need.

Pacing is very natural to a camel, as it is for a giraffe. It's a medium-speed movement where the two legs on the one side move forward, and then the two legs on the other. It sets up a swaying, rolling motion. Many people say it makes them feel 'seasick'. Others liken it to being in a rocking chair — moving sideways!

Neck and head

The camel can lower its long, curved neck in order to eat or drink without kneeling, or stretch it to a height of 3.5 metres — very helpful for leaf nibbling.

Its eyes are protected from the hot blasts of sun and sand by a deep bushy brow. Also shielding the eyes from grit is a double set of long, curly eyelashes. If grains of dust or sand do creep through the eyelashes, an extra, thin inner eyelid winks across the pupil to cleanse it. A camel can shut this eyelid and still see in a sandstorm. Camels have very good vision, both day and night. Special glands supply the eyes with water to keep them moist.

A camel's ears are small and furry, which means sand can't easily get in. A camel has good hearing, but like a donkey, it may choose whether it wants to pay attention to commands or not!

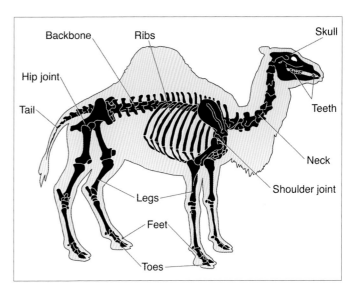

Camel skeleton.

With its hooded eyes, long eyelashes, slanted nostrils and rounded ears, this dromedary can well afford to smile! It's highly suited to its desert environment.

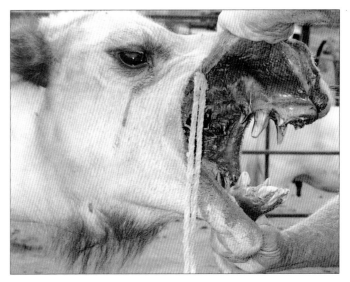

A camel has a large mouth and 34 strong, sharp teeth.

It's not a skin problem! The fur on this dromedary is almost at the end of its moult.

Colours of camels range from cream, light brown, to red and near black, like this one. White or albino camels are rare.

Camels may huddle together to keep cool, because their blood temperature is lower than the hot air temperature.

When the wind whips sand about, the camel can close its slitted nostrils, but still leave small holes through which to breathe. When the storm dies down, it opens them again.

Hump

A camel looks lumpy because of a hump on its back. Some people think it's a water supply, but it's really the camel's larder. It's a boneless mound of fat used by the camel for energy when there's little to eat. As the food store is used up, the hump shrinks and may even fall to one side. Once the camel has eaten again, the hump plumps up.

Coat

Unlike the splotchy colours of giraffes, camels have an all-over colour in their fine fur. Most dromedaries are a sandy, light brown, or 'camel-coloured', similar to the outback environment.

Camels have a winter coat to keep them warm during frosty nights. When that coat moults, or falls off, around springtime, the camel looks scruffy with tufty patches. Clumps of camel wool are found stuck on bushes or fences where the animal has rubbed itself. Around autumn, before the camel grows its new coat, it looks sleek and smooth.

KEEPING COOL AND SAVING WATER

When we get 'goosebumps', our hair stands on end. Camels' hair can stand on end too, but for a different reason. Upright hair allows air to pass through, which evaporates moisture from the skin. Evaporation helps keep the camel cool.

Evaporation helps to keep all animals, including humans, cool when they sweat. But for creatures to keep well and healthy, that moisture has to be replaced. Therefore, they need to drink often. A camel, on the other hand, sweats very little. Its body temperature can raise 3°C above normal without it having the need to sweat. Consequently, water is conserved without the animal suffering. It later releases the stored-up heat at night when it's cooler.

The amount of water a camel drinks depends on the season. During winter it obtains much of its water from succulent plants, but it will drink 30 – 40 litres every day if available and needed. In normal circumstances, however, a camel can go for days and even weeks without drinking. When this happens, the camel's body has to use the water already in its blood and tissues to keep it functioning. The blood naturally thickens, but providing the camel eventually finds water again, it doesn't harm the animal. It would be impossible for humans and other animals to live with such sticky blood.

Extremely thirsty camels can drink about 100 litres or 400 glasses of water in a minute or two. Ten minutes later, their stomachs can be empty, because the water returns immediately to the blood and tissues, replacing all that was lost. However, if feral camels cannot find enough juicy vegetation or surface water, during extreme or ongoing drought, they may die.

A camel's urine is concentrated, because it passes very little water when it pees. The droppings from a dehydrated camel are so dry they can be used immediately for fuel. Desert dwellers rely on this for cooking and heating.

When we breathe out, we lose water as air vapour. The camel saves water because the same membranes in the nasal space that cool incoming warm air also collect moisture when the camel exhales. Tiny blood vessels in the membranes then take it back into the blood. Any water that drips from its nose, however, travels back into its mouth.

CONTROLLING HEAT

On very hot days, camels use little energy, resting rather than feeding, and facing the sun so the smallest surface areas are exposed. Camels may also huddle close together because their blood temperature is lower than the hot air temperature.

The hump acts as a good insulator, especially when the sun is overhead. Because it's large and made up of fat, the movement of heat is restricted. Even its mounded shape is an advantage. If the camel's store of fat was spread around its body, as it is with other animals, it would act as a thick quilt, causing the camel's temperature to rise.

FEEDING

Unfortunately, there are no convenient outback cafes for camels! They have to work hard for their food. Aerial surveys have proved that camels browse for distances of up to 70 kilometres per day.

Using strong teeth, powerful jaws and split upper lip, camels pull at leaves, stems and plants. Because of their tough, thick lips and hardness of the roof of their mouth, they are untroubled by spines or thorny vegetation. Whereas we chew with an up-and-down movement, a camel chews sideways, and then swallows half-chewed food. This goes into one section of the animal's three-section stomach. Later, it will be regurgitated and chewed again, enabling the camel to get the maximum food value. Cud-chewing animals, like camels, deer and cattle, are called ruminants.

Camels eat a variety of food and prefer it fresh. However, being browsers, they only eat a little of one plant before shifting to another. In Australia, camels eat the fruit, leaves and stems from many trees and shrubs, including mulga, spinifex, saltbush and pigweed, as well as honey from grevillea flowers and red fruits from holly leaf grevillea. They'll eat grasses, particularly after rain when they're full of moisture, but grass is their least favourite food.

It's not unusual to find camels browsing around salt lakes or eating salty plants. Camels need salt in their diet to prevent illnesses like skin problems and lameness. Domestic camels are given salt licks.

Unfortunately, at times, camels cause damage to native vegetation, like the quandong or native peach tree, and eat plants that are food and sheltering places for native animals. They also eat plants that are poisonous to them. During one expedition, a camel handler noted in his diary,

> I have to watch out for the heartleaf poison bush that grows in small gullies and so I was kept occupied shepherding the camels. A gut full of that would be the end of the camel.

Very hungry camels will eat charcoal, bones, shoes, rope, meat and even tents!

Pellets of camel dung.

Working camels don't browse as much as feral camels. Instead, they're hand-fed bulky food like hay, dry grains or processed pellets as well as grass, like lucerne. But any change of diet is done gradually to allow the camel to adapt and not get sick.

THE NATURE OF THE CAMEL

Are camels gentle or snappy creatures? Many camel handlers believe that if a camel is treated firmly, fairly, and not trained through fear, it will become calm, friendly and possibly affectionate. It's not always the case, however, and a camel may still prove stubborn at times, grunting and grumbling loudly if it considers it's being treated badly or expected to lift too heavy a load.

A camel does not intentionally spit at people. However, it might have in its mouth a large amount of green cud from its stomach to chew. If it's then hurt or upset, it might growl and cause the smelly mixture to spurt out in a stream. An experienced handler recognises the warning growl and lets the camel relax so it can swallow the cud.

Some camels use their powerful jaws to bite and need to be muzzled on occasions, but most problems come from wild camels, or male camels during the mating season.

Camels sometimes perform a 'happy dance' where they fling their legs about. But occasionally, and for no apparent reason, they kick out, and in any direction. A problem occurs if someone is nearby!

REPRODUCTION

On average, camels live to 50 years old. The male camel is called a bull, the female, a cow, and the baby, a calf.

In Australia, bulls and cows generally mate between April and September, but mating also depends on the season: whether much rain has fallen and how much food is around.

In the wild, a strong bull will live by himself or with other males, but during the rutting season, when he is ready to mate, he will either take over a herd consisting of cows and weaker males, or he'll split the group and form a new herd.

The aggressive appearance of these two frothing male camels (bulls) displays their readiness to mate.

A camel giving birth.

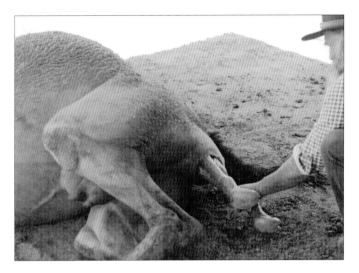

Some gentle help is needed.

All bulls pee backwards. But before mating, a bull will swish his urine-soaked tail onto his rump. He hopes his scent is appealing, and will attract a mate!

During rutting, all bulls become aggressive, restless and almost uncontrollable. A bull will lower his head and stick his neck out to chase away a rival bull that wants to mate with his cow. If the rival remains, the bulls will fight. They stand in a hostile posture, with back legs splayed like a large wishbone. They puff out a peculiar bladder from the side of their mouths and make a hollow, roaring-gurgling noise that can be heard for miles around. White froth lathers from their mouths, and a dark, smelly substance trickles from glands by their ears. Using their strong jaws and teeth, each bull tries to bite the head of the other, or bring it to its knees.

The calf is born.

The defeated bull will leave the area, while the triumphant bull mates with the cow. Afterwards it may either remain with the herd, or also leave. Younger or weaker bulls in the herd may try to mate with cows later in the season.

The pregnant cow carries a single calf for about 13 months before going off alone to give birth. Around the time of the birth, she lowers herself and lies on her side. The calf utters a soft 'baa-aa' much like a lamb, and although feeble, is usually able to stand up by the end of the day. It is born with a soft, woolly coat, but with no hump, and continues to rely on suckling from its mother for a year or longer. During this time, the cow will guard her calf carefully. Large wedgetailed eagles and dingoes prey on weak or wandering calves. The mother and her calf will stay together for many years unless they are forcibly separated.

Camel calves resting.

MUSTERING AND CAPTURE

Where would you find a camel? In a zoo or safari park perhaps. Certainly in a camel farm or at a breeding depot. However, most herds of free-range camels are found in the dry, arid areas of Western Australia, the Northern Territory, western Queensland and northern South Australia.

They're likely to be found near salt lakes, where there's new plant growth, around clay pans, in lightly wooded areas and on top of hills or ranges.

CATCH A CAMEL?

With the thousands of feral camels in Australia, it shouldn't be difficult to catch a camel, should it? But according to one camel handler, catching camels is hard work. 'It's a lot harder than rounding up cattle. Camels are clever animals.' After thirty years of chasing, catching and sending camels overseas, he says, 'they still defy us'. How do you find them? One camel handler explains how he musters with a helicopter:

We fly a search pattern with the chopper to find them. In the desert areas where there are no fences we develop a set pattern, like an ever-increasing circle. In areas where it's fenced you get property maps and work out where everything is and then set out a search pattern to suit that particular area. It's important the chopper pilot has a lot of animal knowledge. Sometimes if I am using pilots that have not mustered camels before I'll run them through on what to do. Like when to push the camels or how to turn them. Sometimes we might need to keep groups separate or bring them together. The spotter is nearly always me. I love flying and it can take a fairly trained eye to locate camels in the remote areas that we search.

The camels take a little while to be educated with the chopper. Once we locate a mob we use the chopper to make them turn a few times so they understand what we want and then we will head them off in the general direction of where we want them to go. At times the chopper is very low to the ground and it's all very exciting and sometimes quite dangerous. Then we move the camels in the direction of the trap, which is hidden in the dunes or the bush. The

A helicopter musters camels into portable holding yards. Hessian 'wings', in the background, help guide the animals into the yard.

The pale brown area of this map shows the distribution of the camel (*Camelus Dromedarius*) in Australia in 1995.

An aerial view showing mustering camels by truck.

trick here is not to let them see or feel that they are being run into portable yards until they are all but there.

By now the camels are tiring and therefore easier to handle. The portable yards are steel panels that are simply fixed together. Wings of hessian, about 100 metres long, are set up to direct the camels into the yards.

The camels then have to be settled down a bit and we do this by leaving them in small yards to get used to humans, lots of noise (cars, bikes, sitting on the side of the yards and talking to them) and heaps of visual activity (we will camp by them, so lots of general noise and camp fires).

Camels are also mustered by motorbike, four-wheel-drive vehicles or by horses. They are less stressed by a horse muster. Trap yards are also used for capturing feral camels. They are set up around a watering point and camels are trapped when they come to drink.

After mustering, we load them onto trucks and deliver them to whoever requires them. Camels are not real keen on walking up a steel cattle race onto the trucks so we will, if we can, dig the back wheels of the truck into the sand and then build a race that is mostly sand and not a very steep incline.

The hollow sound of ramps normally spooks camels, but now, in Alice Springs, camels are being trained to cross ramps by a food reward system. This proven method has the potential to speed up loading camels onto trucks, trains, ships or aeroplanes for export. Fewer camel handlers are required and the need to urge camels along with electric prodders is reduced.

Camels selected for exportation fly sky-high aboard an aeroplane.

Camels in a crate being lifted aboard a ship.

Camels need room to sit when being transported in road trains. Due to their height, they can only be transported in single-deck trailers.

The camel can be loaded directly onto the truck without the use of a ramp, because the truck's wheels have been dug lower into the sand.

CAMEL TRAINING

'Hoosh!' commands the trainer. The camel folds its legs in a stiff, jerky way and sits. Camels must be trained to obey instructions and to accept a saddle, rider and possibly a pack or load. They're big animals and without training, difficult to control. Once trained, they're used for rides, safaris, racing, as pets, or sent to zoos interstate or overseas.

A feral camel can be trained after capture, but the training of a young domestic camel begins when it's about three. By four or five, its bones are strong enough to take a rider or carry a pack.

Camels are curious creatures but easily frightened and feral camels are completely unused to humans. During

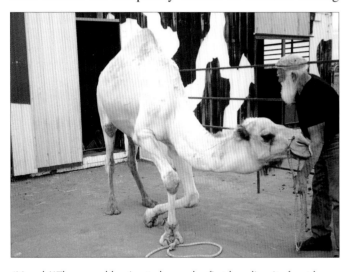

'Hoosh!' The camel begins to lower, by first bending its front leg.

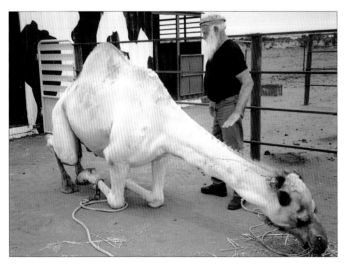

With both front legs down, the back legs are then lowered.

training, the animal should always know who's in charge. Therefore, if the trainer speaks softly, is firm, patient, makes no sudden movements and doesn't hit or beat the animal, he or she will win its confidence.

To get the camel to concentrate, a trainer will work with the animal for only short periods of time, in a yard or area sectioned off and away from other camels. A camel trainer from central Australia says it's necessary that camels have a break during training, 'otherwise they go sour. When they've had enough, they'll just sit down and won't do anything.'

To break in, or tame, a feral camel, one trainer *bags* it first. That is, he uses a bag on the end of a pole to run over the camel's body. The camel grows accustomed to being touched, at a safe distance from the trainer. Next the trainer rotates his hands in front of the camel's face, as if to *mesmerise* it. Then, if the animal is calm, he'll attempt to touch it. If the camel is kicking, however, he'll tie it to a fence or tree and continue to move the sheepskin up close until the animal quietens.

METHODS OF TRAINING

No trainer uses exactly the same methods as another, although there are likely to be similarities. Here are two examples of teaching the command to *sit*:

Method 1: Throw a rope over the camel's shoulder and tie it around the front foot. Pull the rope, until the front

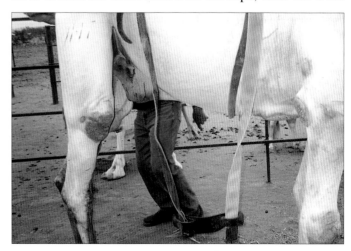

To secure the saddle, girth straps are passed under the camel's belly and buckled.

The saddle is checked for comfort and position.

foreleg drops to the ground and the camel lowers to a sitting position. Say *Hoosh!* so the camel learns to connect the two things.

Method 2: Pull the camel's neck down with the lead rope. Tap in front of the camel's feet. Keep pulling the rope and tapping until the camel sinks. Ease up on the rope and say, *Hoosh!* or *Sit!*

Both the method of instruction and the tone of voice that a trainer uses have to be consistent, so the camel knows what's expected. One camel owner from the Northern Territory commands *Hoosh!* for sit, *Up!* for stand, *Hi-e-ya!* for fast, and *Libera* for slow.

By pulling on the reins or string from the nose peg, a rider can tell the camel which direction to turn. During early sessions, one trainer ties the camel up 'behind the bull camel, and takes him out in the paddock with a long enough string, so then I can steer the camel left and right'. Later she takes the camel out alone.

Getting a camel to accept a saddle on its back can be a difficult job unless the trainer does it gradually. Otherwise, it's scary for a camel and too difficult for the trainer. The trainer might begin by patting or stroking the camel's shoulders or flanks, then later draping a blanket over its back, and eventually adding a bag of stones or sandbags, so the camel feels a heavier weight. Once the camel appears comfortable, the saddle is put on.

In 29 BC, the Romans used camels in chariot races!

With reins in hands and feet in stirrups, Noel Fullerton is ready for a camel ride!

Dust flies as a camel races down a sandhill.

In some ways, camel equipment is different to that used on other domestic animals. To start with, the camel has a hump, so its saddle is an unusual shape. It's a cud-chewing animal, so it can't have a bit in its mouth for guiding, like a horse. Instead, it has a nose peg. And it can wander at night while feeding, so it needs hobbles, or chains.

SADDLES

Camels were one of the earliest animals to be domesticated by humans. Men made saddles so that strong creatures could carry a rider or cart heavy loads.

Afghan cameleers built pack-saddles using available materials, mostly timber, branches and hessian. The frame was a construction of two crosspieces of timber with a bundle of straight branches roped to either side. Saddles were made of hessian or goatskin, and stuffed with various types of straw, even beer-bottle packing.

Nose peg, reins, blanket, saddle and stirrups — all part of the equipment needed to ride a camel. The saddlebag is for carrying goods.

One frame had to fit camels of different sizes and shapes, so the timber had to be strong but flexible. In the early days, working camels carried loads anywhere from 300 to 600 kilograms. Carrying heavy or uneven loads with a saddle that constantly rubbed or bruised the camel's back was both cruel to the animal and bad camel handling. The camel might try to throw the load, refuse to continue or become too injured to work. No cameleer could risk losing an animal or business; it took six or seven years before a young camel was ready to start work. During long journeys, the straw packing in the saddle shifted or was ground down and needed reshaping to keep it firm and comfortable.

Modern saddles have a leather seat. Their frames are made of rounded steel and often moulded to the exact shape of the camel. Before a camel is saddled, a blanket is placed over its back. Too many blankets, however, will make the camel hot and lead to 'scalding', or patchy, discoloured hair.

NOSE PEGS

Domesticated camels wear a nose peg. This is a small wooden or plastic peg with a disk at the back. It's inserted into one of the camel's nostrils and, with the addition of a light rope or string, is used to guide the camel and make it obey instructions. The rope, however, needs to be able to break easily, especially if it's used to connect another camel in a line, or 'string'. If the camel in front jerks suddenly, through anger or fear, the rope connecting the two animals will snap and not tear the nostril of the following camel.

To insert the nose peg, cameleers of old held the camel down on its side, but now special holding gates make the job simpler. A peg hole is made with a skewer or punch and done in an area of the nostril where there are few veins — so there's little or no bleeding — something like getting an earring stud! The hole is treated with antiseptic and fly repellent, and the peg is inserted when the hole has healed.

Old wooden nose pegs were still available in the 1970s at the Oodnadatta general store in South Australia.

The camel owner pushes a nose peg through a hole made in the camel's nostril.

An old Afghan camel saddle.

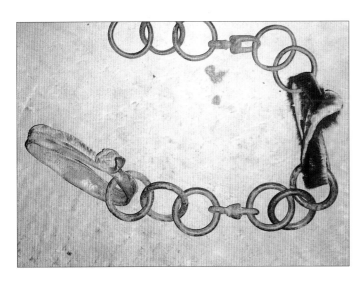

Chain and rawhide hobbles.

HOBBLES

Camels' feet are hobbled, or chained loosely, during overnight camps, otherwise the camels continue to feed and could be kilometres away by morning. Sometimes, early explorers or outback pioneers perished because their camels disappeared like that overnight. Left to the mercy of the desert, the men subsequently died from exhaustion, hunger, heat or thirst.

Early hobbles were made of rawhide leather with a metal chain. Hobbles shouldn't chafe or hurt the animal in any way. If a camel is tethered to a tree instead of being hobbled, the rope needs to be tied around one of its feet, not its neck. During the night, the camel may circle the tree, eating the leaves, until the rope is shortened. Once a camel begins to sit, it has to lower itself completely before it's able to rise again. If the rope is short, the camel might strangle itself.

BELLS

Bells hung around camels' necks made it possible for the early cameleers to detect the animals' whereabouts, and it's said the Afghans could even determine the distance by the tone of the bells, referring to them as the 'one-mile-bell' or the 'two-mile-bell'.

Normally camels follow a lead camel, the one most able to find food. So cameleers often put a bell around its neck, knowing the rest of the herd would stay close.

The author seated on a camel, ready to ride!

HISTORY OF CAMELS IN AUSTRALIA

'Why would any sturdy Britisher want to have anything to do with those outlandish creatures?'

'Too costly to import!'

'Explorers would lose their lives if they used camels instead of horses. How would they cross the floods that the interior is subject to?'

It was attitudes such as these that delayed the early importation of camels and their handlers into South Australia and further inland. Yet it was at Beltana in the same state that the largest, most well-known and respected camel stud in Australia began in 1866.

WHY WERE CAMELS BROUGHT INTO AUSTRALIA AT ALL?

More than half of the continent is arid or semi-arid. Deserts of stony plains or giant sand-dunes are unproductive and difficult to cross. But in the early days of European coastal settlement, the pioneers hoped the vast interior contained rivers and forests, tall mountains and lush valleys. That it might be barren was unthinkable, but was it a possibility?

So, how could the centre's well-kept secret be revealed? Ex-soldiers, who'd served in India but settled in Australia, suggested using camels as transport. At first people scoffed because they'd always relied on the familiar horses and bullocks, but in 1839, a Sydney newspaper reported that camels were animals 'admirably adapted to the climate and soil of New South Wales'.

THE FIRST AUSSIE CAMELS

Three camels arrived in Australia one year later. A pair, a male and a female, arrived in Tasmania aboard the *Calcutta*. Crowds thronged to see the strange creatures. Their owner, Mr J. Ardlie, put them on show before shipping them to be displayed in Melbourne. Later they were overlanded to Sydney — the first Australian camel trek ever. A calf was

Here, a camel is transferred in a sling, onto the wharf at Port Augusta in South Australia.

A camel train plods across flat plains carrying wool bales and firewood.

A team of camels pulls a cart carrying sandalwood in Western Australia.

born and the New South Wales Government bought all three for £225 and exhibited them in the Sydney Domain.

Pastoralist and explorer John Horrocks of Clare, South Australia, owned the third camel. It was the only survivor of a batch shipped from the Canary Islands. Horrocks used it when travelling north in search of good land. Unfortunately, the camel accidentally jolted Horrocks as he held a loaded gun. It fired and injured Horrocks, who died three weeks later. Earlier he'd requested the camel be destroyed, as he was concerned about its future.

Around 1860, three further camels arrived in Melbourne. Actor and showman George Coppin exhibited them and used them in performances, but nothing is known of the animals' fate.

In June 1860, over two dozen camels and three handlers arrived in Melbourne aboard the *Chinsurah* to assist the explorers Robert Burke and William Wills on an expedition across the continent.

However, it was two South Australians, Samuel Stuckey and Thomas Elder who, in 1866, began the business of importing large numbers of camels to Australia. The early settlements in the inland didn't have a neat, easy connection of townships. Rather, they were spread out, like small islands dotted in oceans of red sandhills, saltbush and gibber plains. Somehow, goods had to reach the people, while wool, wheat and minerals had to be carted back to ports or the closest point of a railway.

Stuckey had visited India in 1862 to assess the camel's value and its possible use in Australia. Thomas Elder, a wealthy pastoralist, was keen to establish camels on his properties. He'd been impressed with explorer John McKinlay's admirable account of camels he'd used during his search for the missing explorers Burke and Wills.

SHIPS OF THE DESERT

At the time when Elder and Stuckey began business discussions, the inland was suffering from a long and severe drought. Not only were stock dying but there was no water or vegetation for transport horses or bullocks to eat along the way.

It was a desperate time. Could camels prove themselves to be 'ships of the desert' in Australia and deliver the much-needed goods to the inland?

Stuckey and Elder were spurred into action. On a warm

A camel at Beltana, the place of one of the oldest camel studs in Australia.

New Year's Day in 1866, over 120 camels and 31 camel handlers arrived from Karachi, India, aboard the steamship *Blackwall*, and docked at Port Augusta in South Australia.

Several camels had died on the voyage and several female camels were pregnant, but the camels had been chosen either for carting or carrying, or for riding. An excited crowd gathered on the wharf to watch the animals being off-loaded. An account of the camels was reported in *The Advertiser*, a South Australian newspaper:

> *Mr Stuckey was to tie their legs, and being placed in a sling, more like a bundle of merchandise than a living animal, they were then lowered into the punts, seven or eight in each punt and passed on to the shore by a warp. As soon as they walked out of the barges, those that did not feel sea-groggy about the legs indulged in some frolicsome antics.*

Immediately the camels were loaded with goods, they were led to Umberatana, one of Elder's northern stations. Stuckey was delighted to watch the camels' condition improve, in spite of the drought-stricken countryside. Those animals later formed part of the Beltana camel stud.

Before Elder and Stuckey set up a camel transport company in 1869, Elder had already trained the camels to do without water for extended periods. Strings of camels then began the goods-carrying business between Port Augusta in South Australia, and distant settlements, often returning with loads of wool and copper.

Beltana camels were used during the construction of the Overland Telegraph Line, and by a number of exploration parties. In 1875, the explorer Ernest Giles used camels in his expedition from South Australia to Perth in Western Australia. At one stretch, the camels travelled 220 miles (352 kilometres) in 8 days before Giles found water for them. After a further 12 days of travelling, he gave them each a bucket of water. That remarkable feat publicised the quality and stamina of the animals.

Though other camel depots developed, particularly in Western Australia and Queensland, Beltana camels had a high reputation and were exported to all states, except Victoria and Tasmania, and to Arabia.

In 1870, disputes arose between Elder and a group of

Camels are part of the scene of an early settler's camp. In the background, a waterbag and a meat safe hang beneath the brushwood shelter which shades a table, incongruously set with a white tablecloth.

Growing up with camels. Allan Homes and friend in the 1940s at Marree in South Australia. Allan's pet camel is a descendent of one of the 6000 camels that worked the area for many years.

Bedecked in their fine clothes and hats, these ladies and gentlemen set out on an outing. Ladies mostly rode side-saddle.

Families in the outback rode camels from place to place. This family is setting out from 'Callana', west of Marree around 1910.

Afghan cameleers whom he'd employed. Many left Beltana and some, like Faiz and Tagh Mahomet (or Mahomed), set up their own camel business. In 1884, the Mahomets brought out a large shipment of 293 camels and 56 handlers to carry goods to the Western Australian goldfields.

Between 1860 and 1907, an estimated 10,000 to 12,000 camels were imported from India and Pakistan, as there was a need for a large number of cheap animals. Most were the heavier, draught camels but a small number of a fine riding type, similar to a thoroughbred, was thought to have been imported from the Sudan. By the late 1800s, basic quarantine measures were in operation, requiring camels to be kept in isolation for thirty days at the port of entry.

Under the guidance of Afghan cameleers, many Aborigines and Europeans became expert camel handlers. They worked chiefly in local areas, while the Afghans dominated the use of camels for cartage, or freight transportation, over long distances. Many large strings of

Dromedaries from India and Pakistan adapted well to Australian conditions.

A government camel team.

Camel owner Archie Kite, district nurse Mavis Wilson and Aboriginal tracker Mickey with a camel wagon carting wood at Marree.

camels consisted of 70 camels and four Afghan handlers. Harnessing a team of camels to a wagon meant twice the load could be carried, without the burdensome loading and unloading at the end of a day. Camels were also hitched to buggies, or ridden for general purposes. Women often rode side-saddle as it was considered more ladylike.

The last importation of camels was at Port Hedland, Western Australia, in 1907. Vehicles arrived in the outback after World War I, around the 1920s and 30s, and the need for camel transport came to a sudden, sad end, although the use of camels in survey work and explorations continued past the 1930s, and they were used for police work, well into the 1950s.

With no work for their animals, and often unable to pay the high government fee for registration, many Afghans released their camels into the wild rather than

see them destroyed. Those freed camels bred, and that's how Australia came to be the home of the only wild herds of dromedaries in the world, with hundreds of thousands of these extraordinary creatures roaming the inland. The camels are strong and healthy, but their original purpose has gone. Today they are considered a valued tourist attraction and export animal.

During an expedition in Antarctica in 1911, the famous Australian explorer Sir Douglas Mawson, used a sleeping bag padded with camel hair.

Camels to the rescue! A bogged car being pulled out of the sand in the 1920s.

From work to pleasure; nowadays camels are part of the outback tourist industry.

THE AFGHAN CAMEL MEN

Imagine walking along desert sand so hot it heats up the nails in your shoes! Wearing boots with no socks, the hardy, independent Afghan cameleers trudged with their camels for months at a time, along stock routes and tracks spanning three-quarters of the Australian continent.

Often the routes were of the men's making. They considered the best walking paths for their animals, and the presence of waterholes. At stopping places, they planted date seeds, which grew into palms and later provided a welcome and familiar food souce.

The Afghans and their camels were vital to outback life. They were involved in rescue operations, explorations, police tracking, laying railways and telegraph lines, erecting fences, carrying mail, ploughing dams, setting up water pumps and bores, and hauling supplies to, and wool from, remote pastoral stations.

But who were these incredible men, who arrived by ship from far-off countries? Most spent the voyage living with their camels in the dark holds of steamships, emerging to step out on to new soil dressed in baggy pants, loose shirts, wide cummerbunds and turbans.

What a spectacle they must have seemed to the nineteenth-century, white, Anglo-Saxon Australians. The cameleers were exotic, dark-skinned men who smelled of camels and Eastern fragrant oils. They spoke the Pushtu language and had little or no knowledge of English. The majority were devout Muslims. They brought their own Islamic religion and culture into Australia, a country which at the time hadn't even recognised its own Aboriginal history.

They'd been offered jobs as camel handlers to work in the outback of Australia for up to four years. They were not allowed to bring their wives and families. Up to 4,000 were said to be living in Australia during the heyday of camel transport, between the 1860s and 1920s.

The men were called Afghans. Most of them, however, were not from the area called Afghanistan in central Asia. Many were from the Indian northwest frontier, in what is now Pakistan; others were from Baluchistan, towards Iran; while still others were from Arabia, Egypt and Turkey.

Men, with names like Bejah Dervish, Charlie Sadadeen, Fazzledine and Fayid Mulladad, came from regions of northern India, Pakistan and Afghanistan to work as cameleers in Australia. They were paid £2 per month.

An Afghan at prayer near Alice Springs, Northern Territory, in 1934. Most cameleers had a special prayer mat to kneel on, but a clean sheet or towel would do.

Despite that, dark-skinned people who worked with camels in those days were called Afghans.

For over 70 years, the cameleers' cries rang out. *'Hoosh! Hoosh! Hooshta!'* The camels would groan noisily as they sat and waited to be loaded. A large bull camel could carry 600 kilograms, while an average camel carried 240 kilograms. They'd travel for eight hours a day, up to two months at a time. The men were expert in loading the camels quickly and balancing the loads evenly. Because it was a tough and time-consuming job, the Afghans didn't stop for a midday meal. That would have meant unloading and reloading the camels. During the day though, the men would stop to pray, and then walk on until it was time to camp in the evening.

After the camels were unloaded, they were left to rest and chew their cud. Later the handlers chained the animals' legs with special hobbles or loose chains to prevent them wandering off during the night. The men sheltered under tarpaulins or beside ridges of sand or rock. They sang, ate, repaired saddles or made rawhide pads for the camels' feet if the route was very rocky.

Besides carting goods, cameleers needed to transport their own provisions and basic equipment. One camel carried water for the men in wooden or metal containers, and was called the 'water camel'. At deep wells, cameleers dropped a tin bucket down to draw water for their camels. Sometimes the wells were dry or covered with sand, but at permanent settlements, like Beltana, there was a camel whirl or whip, where camel power was used to raise and lower buckets from a well.

The 'kitchen camel' carried food and kitchen supplies. According to Muslim tradition, the Afghans only ate meat that had been killed *al halal* — meat killed by another Muslim, preferably a mullah or priest. He would face the beast in the direction of Mecca, the Muslims' holy city in Saudi Arabia, and complete a prayer prior to slaughtering. Live goats were taken on journeys for fresh meat.

Each Afghan kept a change of clothes, small personal items and a prayer mat in a camel pack-saddle. The Afghans who first came to Australia were strict about their daily prayers, which they performed on mats facing Mecca. The teaching of the Qur'an (Koran), the Islamic holy book, advocates five prayers daily. However, it is believed that many cameleers felt three was acceptable while in Australia. On their long journeys, sometimes there was not enough water to cleanse themselves before prayers, so they'd run their hands through sand.

An Afghan cameleer pours a welcome drink of water from a canvas bag into a tin cup.

Children on a camel at Marree in South Australia, at a town reunion in the 1970s. The old Afghan mosque is in the background.

Muslims are forbidden to drink alcohol. Therefore the cameleers could be trusted to deliver any load of strong drink without touching a drop. But they refused to eat or carry any pig meat, such as pork, ham or bacon. According to Muslim tradition, the pig is considered an unclean animal. This custom, among others, set Afghans apart from many others in the community. It caused food problems and conflicts on journeys or expeditions and became the topic of jokes played on Afghans and their families. One descendant remembered that her childhood in Marree was often unhappy, because 'people used to make fun of us, put pigs on our turnstile.'

If an Afghan died at a distance from his home or mosque, his long, white turban was unwound and used as a shroud. His gravestone, whether placed in a cemetery or not, would face Mecca.

Afghans settled where there was work, mostly near mines and railheads. But they lived separately from the rest of the community, often in makeshift iron and tarpaulin houses with their Aboriginal or European wives. These collections of homes and bush mosques came to be known as Ghan Towns. Eventually many Ghan Towns were scattered throughout the country, from Port Augusta in South Australia to Alice Springs in the Northern Territory, Port Hedland to Kalgoorlie, throughout New South Wales and as far north as Townsville in Queensland. The first city mosque was in Adelaide. Later, others were built in Perth, Broken Hill, Sydney and Alice Springs.

Afghans had special ceremonies. After a religious period of fasting, the Afghans feasted around a camp fire. The air would be filled with aromas of goat curries, chapattis, sweets, dates and nuts. The men, dressed in their best loose shirts, baggy pants and embroidered tunics, sang, danced and smoked from a long-stemmed water-smoking pipe.

The Afghans were often subject to prejudice and outrage. They were hard workers, offering fast, reliable service, yet there were clashes with other carters. Bullocky drivers and horse teamsters accused Afghans of undercutting prices and ruining their businesses, even though their animals might not have been able to navigate or endure the same routes as the camels. During periods of low employment, Afghans were also blamed for seizing white people's jobs, but cameleering was a lonely, arduous job. Many white men

Afghans unloading wool from Nappamerri Station, Queensland, at Farina railway station, South Australia in 1928.

The railway line at Marree divided the inhabitants. Europeans lived on one side and Afghan cameleers and their families on the other. Each cameleer had a camel yard next to his home.

Jessie Fullerton, a descendant of an Afghan cameleer.

didn't want it, or couldn't do it. It was work that the majority of Australians living in coastal areas knew little about.

When the Afghans' contracts ended, a large number returned to their homelands. Those who remained found other work or formed their own camel-carting companies. During the 1890s, Abdul Wade had over 400 camels and 60 Afghan drivers, while Gool Mahomet (Mahomed) and his sons bought Mulgaria Station in South Australia in 1924 and turned it into a camel depot.

Others Afghans became travelling salesmen or hawkers. They filled tarpaulin-covered boxes with all sorts of items, such as pens, packets of cards, boiled sweets, books, boots, dresses, cottons, cheap jewellery and biscuits. After loading them on camels or camel wagons, they'd set off for their six-monthly trip to outlying stations. A hawker's arrival was often like Christmas for the children and families in isolated areas. Sometimes, however, their visits were not welcomed and a 'No Hawkers' or 'No Afghans' sign was displayed.

Sadly, the arrival of motorised vehicles and the railway, during the 1920s and 30s, hastened the end of the camels and the livelihood of their industrious, faithful handlers. Hundreds of animals were set free. As one old Afghan watched his camels disappear over the ridge, he said quietly, 'I say goodbye, my camel'.

The numbers of wild camels grew to such an extent that they were termed pests. The Camel Destruction Act in 1925 meant that pastoralists and government officials had the right to shoot any camels on their property or common ground.

It was a desperate time for those remaining cameleers and their families. Camels had been their life. Many Afghans found it hard to adjust to new work. Some sought work in the new railways and others became farmhands, drivers, horsemen, small property owners and general labourers.

Only one Afghan cameleer was publicly recognised. Mahomet Allum became a well-respected herbalist, healer and spiritual leader of the Muslims, and lived the remainder of his life in Adelaide. Mahomet was not granted Australian citizenship because he was classified as non-white. When the law changed, he didn't re-apply.

The lives of Afghan cameleers, Aborigines and Lutheran missionaries feature in *Serenades*, an outback film released in 2001.

Today there are several significant reminders of the great contribution Afghan cameleers made to the outback of Australia. There are stone markers, or cairns, built by the men to assist navigation around the Birdsville Track: an old stock route that connected Marree in South Australia and Birdsville in Queensland. There are date palms, several mosques, the Ghan train and in 2002, The Last Camel Train re-enactment. The Last Camel Train journey celebrated its arrival in Alice Springs at a park near the Council Chambers. It's been re-named Nishaan-E-Afghan Park which means 'In memory of Afghans'.

Camels and their Afghan handlers left tracks far and wide throughout the continent during their 70 years of service. It was those tracks which settlers, pastoralists and miners followed, opening up the inland as they went.

A section of a mural in Alice Springs, Northern Territory.

IN LOVING MEMORY OF
GOOL MAHOMED
BORN 11. 3. 1908 DIED 28. 5. 1985
AGED 77 YEARS
BELOVED HUSBAND OF BETH
LOVED FATHER TO ALL HIS CHILDREN

SADLY MISSED

THE LAST OF THE ORIGINAL
CAMELEERS

The gravestone of a well-known cameleer in Central Australia.

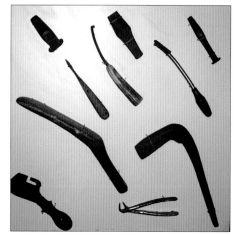

Saddle-making tools that were used by cameleer Sallay Mahomet.

EXPLORERS

What were early Australian explorers looking for? As well as surveying for communication and transport routes between settlements they were also on the look-out for:

- good pastoral land
- reliable water supplies
- minerals.

Largely, their journeys charted country never before seen by Europeans.

Expeditions weren't attempted single-handedly. Explorers chose men and animals considered suitable for the task.

The first explorer to use a camel was South Australian pastoralist John Horrocks. In 1846, he discovered a pass through the Flinders Ranges, later named Horrocks Pass.

The Burke and Wills expedition was the first to use camels in large numbers for transport. In 1860, the government offered a prize of £2000 to the first expedition to cross the continent from south to north. Burke and Wills took horses, 26 camels and four experienced Afghan cameleers: Dost Mahomet, Belooch, Hassan (Esan) Khan and Samla.

There was much to arrange. When one European suggested packing pepper and rum to enliven tired camels the idea was scoffed at, but other preparations included a wagon that converted into a boat; flannel-lined waterproof covers for the camels in wet weather; 'expedition biscuits' (dried, minced meat baked in wheat flour) to sustain the men and two sets of double-folded leather shoes lined with iron for the camels to wear on stony ground.

The shoes did not fit and the expedition ended in tragedy. Despite Burke reaching the northern Gulf of Carpentaria, John King was the sole survivor of the exploration party. Of the six camels used to make the final dash to the northern coast, only four survived. The rest had either strayed or were cut up and eaten after becoming bogged or too exhausted to work.

Unfortunately, the expedition failed to highlight the worthiness of camels in such terrible conditions. However, John McKinlay used horses and camels on one of the search parties for Burke and Wills, (and again on his own transcontinental droving feat of 1861), and praised the camels, saying they were 'undoubtedly the best of all animals for this kind of work'.

Though the continent had been crossed, there was still much land unexplored. Little was known of the centre of Australia or the area west of the Overland Telegraph Line; towards the settled regions of Western Australia.

Explorers were keen to discover more. Colonel Peter Egerton Warburton, Ernest Giles, William Christie Gosse, Albert Calvert, John Lewis, John Ross, William Henry Tietkins, David Lindsay and Charles Winnecke conducted expeditions using camels, preferring those bred at Beltana. Explorers respected and valued the Afghans for their

Camels like browsing on vegetation around salt lakes. However, the sight of such a lake in this aridness would have been a cruel blow to early explorers whose continual search for water was often desperate.

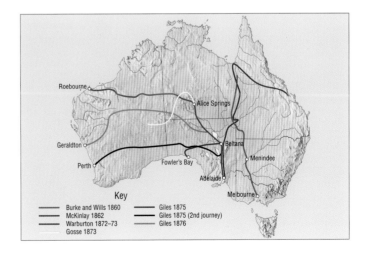

This map shows the routes taken across the inland by explorers and their camels.

remarkable skills in bushmanship and endurance, as well as camel handling. Several explorers named geographical features after the cameleers, including Kamran's Well and Allanah's Hill. However, it was chiefly the work of the explorers that gained public recognition and praise. Little or no mention was made of the vital part the Afghans played.

> Afghan cameleers performed skin grafts by sewing patches of goatskin over the sore backs of their camels.

Day after day, explorers and their parties struggled across unfamiliar, barren country, experiencing terrible hardships. In 1883 Chas Winnecke explored the area around Queensland's border. His diary extracts report:

August, Saturday 25th – no. 7 camp.

The camels . . . managed to stray away about six miles during the night, looking for water, I suppose, which prevented us from getting an early start. It is now about eleven days since they had a good drink.

Monday 27th.

This country is very bad for camels to travel over; the wind has blown the sand into innumerable little hillocks or mounds, over which the camels are constantly stumbling, and, being unable to get a foothold on the slippery spinifex, they now and then have a heavy fall.

Tuesday 28th – No 10 camp.

One of our camels refused to get up this morning: we gave him a little water out of our kegs and a rest before we started.

Friday 31st.

I shall have to stay here tomorrow . . . to give the camels a chance to regain their condition . . . they traversed 205 miles of the heaviest and worst sandhill country in Australia; in reality they have been sixteen days, and travelled 278 miles, without a drink as they would not touch the putrid muck and water at Warman's Well.

Wednesday 5th September.

We crossed . . . Mulligan River . . . which was extremely boggy; the camels only just managed to struggle through, leaving tracks and holes in the lake, which will be visible for years to come.

Warrior, the camel, belonged to Larry Wells, a member of Calvert's 1896-97 expedition across the Great Sandy Desert in Western Australia. Expedition members and the search party suffered appalling hardships in the hot, waterless desert.

Well into the nineteenth century there were still only a few Europeans living in the inland of Australia. Without the Afghans and their camels and the Aborigines' knowledge of the land, the task of opening it up would have been far tougher. All were vital to the construction of the Overland Telegraph Line, the Trans-Australian Railway, the Rabbit-Proof and Dog (Dingo) Proof Fences and the Canning Stock Route.

THE OVERLAND TELEGRAPH LINE

Electric power and telegraphic links were the talk of the world in the early nineteenth century. Australia was a continent isolated from the rest of the world. Ships from England brought news and mail that was months late. Anxious farmers received stale information about wool and wheat prices.

Could a telegraph line be laid across the country and connected to an underground cable already set up in Java, Indonesia? Charles Todd, Postmaster General and Superintendent of Telegraphs, was certain it could. It would be the 'giant electric chain' that linked Australia to the rest of the world.

Todd decided the route of the overland line would follow the tracks of explorer John McDouall Stuart. Stuart had been successful in his third attempt to cross the continent from south to north in 1862. And Todd knew that Stuart had been helped in his trek by Aborigines who had shown him the whereabouts of waterholes and mound springs.

The construction of the south-north telegraph line began in 1870 and was broken up into eleven stages. At each stage, tracks were cut and timber poles felled or carted by camels, and then positioned. Instructions from overseers stated:

The poles may be straight rough gum, pine or stringy bark saplings or other timber not liable to be attacked by white ants. Number of the poles to the mile, twenty. Great care must be taken erecting poles to range them in a straight line.

Camels carried huge loads of wire, water and provisions, as well as hauling heavy stones for building telegraph repeater station huts. The route was forged across hundreds

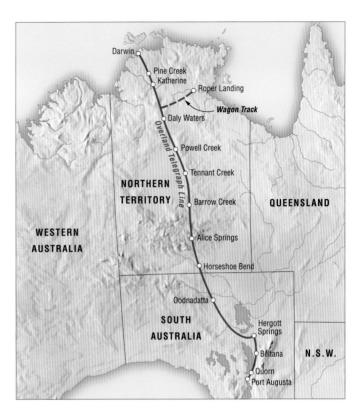

The Overland Telegraph Line. It took two years to stretch this strand of wire on poles across desert, mountain ranges and tropical forest.

of kilometres of unknown land, made more difficult by the flies, heat, lack of water, hostile Aborigines and the extended wait for iron posts to replace the wooden ones eaten by white ants. In the northern regions, tropical forests, prickly heat rashes and mosquitoes added to the problems and discomfort. 'Axemen and others complained that their moist woollen singlets became flyblown and live objects would soon appear . . .' Some men decided to quit, others became ill and six men died during construction.

In 1872, the Overland Telegraph Line was completed. It was a staggering feat of skill and endurance. A total of 36,000 poles were used over 3,200 kilometres, from Port Augusta in South Australia to Darwin in the Northern Territory. Using morse code, Todd tapped out the first message:

We have this day, within two years, completed a line of communication two thousand miles long through the very centre of Australia, until a few years ago a terra incognita [unknown land] believed to be a desert.

Construction of the Overland Telegraph near Marree, South Australia, c. 1871.

The telegraph repeater station at Tennant Creek. Messages were repeated along the rest of the Overland Telegraph.

Carting water during construction of the Trans-Australian Railway, c. 1910.

THE TRANS-AUSTRALIAN RAILWAY

Getting about from place to place is far easier today than it was a hundred years ago. Prior to 1917, there was not even a track spanning the 1,000-mile (1,600-kilometre) east–west stretch between Port Augusta in South Australia and Kalgoorlie, a goldmining town in Western Australia. The trip took eight days by ship. A railway was needed.

In 1908, surveyors from both states drew up plans to peg the best route and meet at the border. Richard J. Anketell, who'd earlier surveyed and built the Rabbit-Proof Fence, led his four-man party east on camels.

It was a demanding, monotonous journey. The men walked or rode 48 kilometres per day across barren country, lived on tinned meat and strict water rations, and did not see another person for the entire three months of the journey. After trudging 720 kilometres they reached the border, only to find the South Australian party had not yet arrived.

They built a limestone cairn, checked latitude and longitude directions, and headed south to Eucla on the coast. There, at the small telegraph repeater station, the men confirmed their bearings, turned their camels and started back to Western Australia along the route they'd pegged.

Before the railway was completed in 1917, camels were an everyday sight along the route. During its construction, camels and their Afghan drivers brought chaff to feed the horses, provisions and water for the men, and equipment and railway sleepers for the track.

THE RABBIT-PROOF FENCE

Originally, there were no rabbits in Australia. But Thomas Austin was a keen hunter. In 1859, he brought 24 wild rabbits over from England and released them on his property near Geelong in Victoria so that he could enjoy the gentlemanly pleasure of shooting. In 1867 he shot 14,362 rabbits on his property alone! It was obvious the animals had adapted well to Australia and had bred abundantly.

Numbers swelled until plagues of rabbits infested Victoria, New South Wales, Queensland and swept across outback Australia towards Western Australia. Soon hundreds of thousands of rabbits were moving like 'a mass of water with grey ripples on it', devastating crops and pasture, and ring-barking trees. Huge numbers invaded country towns and roads, and farmers tried in vain to fence off their properties. It was a grave problem and something had to be done to prevent the rabbits from spreading further into Western Australia.

In 1901, Alfred Canning surveyed a route for a government-constructed, rabbit-proof fence. Richard J. Anketell and his teams of men, using horses, mules and 350 camels then worked hard for seven years to complete the first of three rabbit-proof fences. The first fence stretched for 1,620 kilometres from the south coast near Esperance in Western Australia to Wallal in the northwest. It was the longest anti-rabbit fence in the continent.

From thereon, the fence had to be maintained. Boundary riders, often accompanied by an Aboriginal man, would patrol a section with three pack camels and enough tools, water and provisions for a month. They checked for snakes which often curled up at the base of the fence, clipped back grass, and repaired holes in netting. The big, quiet camels, originally trained by Afghans, were taught to steer clear of the fence because the barbed wire tore at pack-saddles.

Many other fences were built, but they mostly proved unsuccessful. Wombats, rabbits or kangaroos damaged them, or they became buried in sand drifts. Maintenance of large stretches of fencing was difficult and sometimes rabbits got through before a section was complete. Though rabbits stopped at fences, when their numbers were great, they piled up and others simply climbed over them ladder-style!

THE DOG (DINGO) FENCE

Dingoes have always been a menace to livestock. They destroy animals in huge numbers. Before World War II, a shooter or trapper could earn money for killing dingoes by producing the animal's scalp as proof.

Dingoes attack sheep more brutally than cattle, so in 1948, a single-line dog fence was built to protect the sheep. It ran from the Great Australian Bight in southern Australia to Jimbour in south-east Queensland. Stretching 5,400 kilometres across five deserts and two states, it's the longest fence in the world. 'Inside' the fence to the south is sheep-grazing country, which is chiefly free of dingoes. North or 'outside' the fence is cattle country.

In the early days, solitary boundary riders checked sections of the fence by camel. Nowadays, feral camels sometimes cause problems by trampling it.

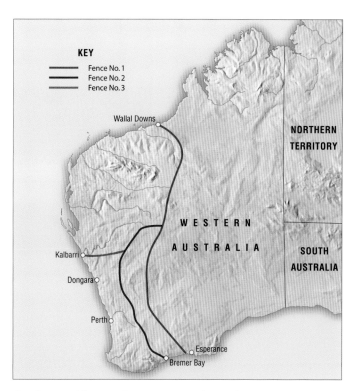

The three Rabbit-Proof Fences. Boundary riders, sometimes with families, were stationed every 40 kilometres. Some rode bicycles when checking the fences but most patrolled by camel.

The Dog Fence is so important that each section is checked every 48 hours. This section is north-east of Coober Pedy in South Australia.

THE CANNING STOCK ROUTE

At the end of the nineteenth century, there was a thriving cattle industry in the Kimberley region of northern Western Australia, but no track existed for the drovers to get the animals to a port in Perth or a market in Kalgoorlie.

In 1906, Alfred Canning surveyed a 1,440-kilometre route through some of the most arid country in Western Australia, from Hall's Creek in the Kimberley Ranges to Wiluna, a railhead in the Murchison area. He led a party of 26 men, with 2 wagons and 62 camels. They also took 800 goats for fresh meat along the way. Afghan camel drivers loaded all equipment and supplies necessary, including materials to make the track and build timber-lined wells. During the two years of construction, 52 wells were dug at a day's droving from each other.

Unfortunately, drovers found the route unsuitable. At times it crossed sandhills 15 metres high, making access impossible for wheeled vehicles. Pack camels were therefore necessary to carry the drovers' provisions. The wells were later to prove too shallow and unreliable for a mob of cattle.

The track was eventually considered unusable and by the early 1950s had fallen into disrepair.

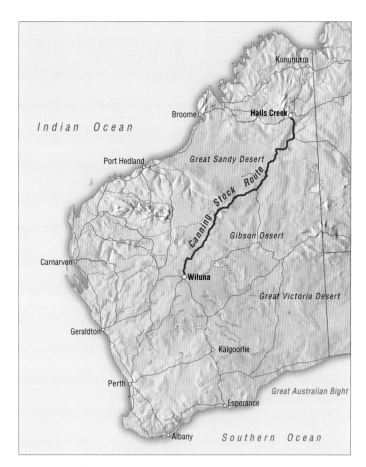

Due to cattle tick, the government prevented cattle from being droved to southern markets. The Canning Stock Route opened up trade because the insects couldn't survive a desert crossing.

In 2003, trains on the east-west railway line knocked down many drought-stricken camels. No rain had fallen on the Nullarbor Plain for two years and the thirsty animals were licking dew off the tracks.

An original steam engine of the old Ghan train at Quorn, South Australia, c. 1920s.

Camel farm owners, Nick and Michelle Smail, with Afghan descendant Eric Sultan, at Alice Springs in the Northern Territory to celebrate the arrival of the Ghan in 2004, which now travels along the longest north-south railway track in the world.

CAMELS AND THE GHAN TRAIN

The steam train 'hissed and snarled, grunted and whistled, and smoked like some monstrous human being'.

It was 1899 and the old Ghan train chugged northwards along the narrow-gauge railway between Port Augusta and the railhead at Oodnadatta in South Australia. Earlier, Hergott Springs (later named Marree) in South Australia had been the railhead, and it wasn't until 1929 that the railway reached Alice Springs in the Northern Territory.

The train travelled through desolate and flood-prone country, which caused constant hold-ups. When it slowed to a snail's pace, passengers got out and walked, because it was cooler than being in the train. Heat buckled the rails and sand drifts buried them. Plagues of grasshoppers caused the carriages to skid off rails, and washaways marooned passengers for days. Obliging engine drivers, however, poured boiling water into passengers' teapots or

billy cans for cups of tea. And passengers could swim in the bore at Coward Springs in South Australia, while the train refilled with water.

The construction of the railway began in 1878 to service inland mines and sheep and cattle properties. It was laid in stages, with camels hauling great loads of railway equipment and supplies. The work party toiled in harsh conditions, frequently hanging lanterns around the camels' necks because the windstorms were so severe.

In 1980 a new line to Alice Springs was completed, but it ran via Tarcoola, 150 kilometres west of the old route.

Twenty-four years later, the rail was extended to Darwin. On 1 February 2004, the first Ghan passenger train left Adelaide on the 2,979-kilometre trip to the northern capital. Once called the Afghan Express, the Ghan train displays an emblem of a camel and rider, a tribute to the Afghan cameleers.

WOOL AND MORE

No place was too far or too isolated for the camels and their Afghan drivers. They'd cart supplies to inland towns, mining camps, Aboriginal settlements and missions, and to outlying sheep and cattle stations.

The goods first had to be railed or carted to a railhead, then sorted and loaded at that crossover. Therefore, said cameleer Sallay Mahomet:

> *The camel camp was always not far from the railway and the agent used to bring this stuff out on a horse trolley every day; cart it all out and drop it there for us to tie up into loads. There'd be flour, sugar, tea and fencing material, barbed wire — plenty of plain wire and plenty of wire netting. Sheets of iron, pipes, rods, whatever you're going to mention on a station property, that's what we carried, everything . . . We had to batch it up into equal sized loads on each camel. Worst stuff was barbed wire.*

Pastoralists used wire to fence huge areas of their sheep stations in an effort to keep out the dingoes which killed or injured sheep. On return trips, camels carried different loads. Sallay Mahomet commented that of all the goods they back-loaded in central Australia,

> *wool was the main heavy load we used to have. Big wool bales — they were good — they were heavy, but they were good loading, they didn't move.*

A sturdy camel with its evenly balanced wool bales weighing about 600 kilograms.

Kilner's Ltd., Oodnadatta removalists! Camels are harnessed to a cart piled high with a family's furniture and belongings.

Camels carting goods belonging to German missionary Liebler and his wife, at Hermannsburg Mission near Alice Springs in 1913.

J. Dance's team from Edugena, Yarri in Western Australia hauls a wagon of bagged wheat.

Historic 'Glen Maggie' in Central Australia depended on camels for its water supply from Ryan's Well. The homestead was built in 1914 and abandoned in 1935, when the telegraph office was moved.

In packing a normal load, two Afghans stood either side of the camel, pulled the ropes and tied up the goods. 'One large wool bale needed four of us to lift him up, right up,' said Sallay Mahomet.

One aspect of wool carting which cameleers disliked was carrying wool full of locks (the dirty part of the sheep . . . the backsides and all the gritty wool), because the extra grit made the wool heavier than normal fleece; and another was carting a round wool bale, because it was difficult loading that shape.

As draught animals, the camels hauled bagged wheat, stacked tall as towers, on top of wagons or drays. In drought-affected areas around Bourke in New South Wales, they pulled transport coaches for the highly successful Cobb & Co. company when horses couldn't. They carried polling boxes

Ryan's Well was one of a number of wells built by Ned Ryan in the late 1880s. Diagram (below) shows how camels helped to raise the water.

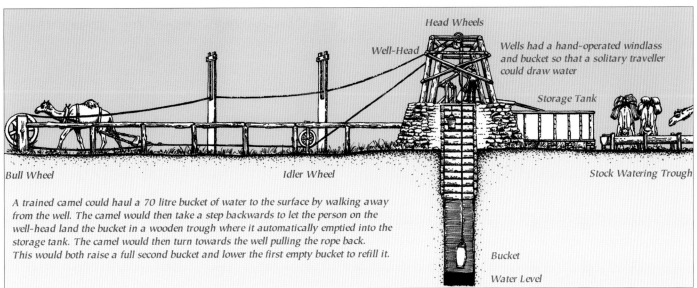

Head Wheels

Well-Head

Wells had a hand-operated windlass and bucket so that a solitary traveller could draw water

Storage Tank

Bull Wheel

Idler Wheel

Stock Watering Trough

Bucket

Water Level

A trained camel could haul a 70 litre bucket of water to the surface by walking away from the well. The camel would then take a step backwards to let the person on the well-head land the bucket in a wooden trough where it automatically emptied into the storage tank. The camel would then turn towards the well pulling the rope back. This would both raise a full second bucket and lower the first empty bucket to refill it.

to outlying areas at election times and after a windstorm, helped scoop sand away from outback homesteads.

What would have happened without the camels?

CAMELS AND MINING

Minerals! It was a word that set men's hearts racing in the early days of European settlement in Australia. It sent explorers, surveyors, geologists, prospectors, miners, adventurers and thousands of others out into the hot, dry inland in search of gold, minerals and precious stones.

Transport was a serious problem until people realised the best animal for the expeditions was the camel. It could venture into areas that neither a horse or bullock could go, or survive in.

As various mines developed throughout the country, strings of these 'ships of the desert' could be seen nose-pegged together, plodding from railheads or shipping ports, with their cargo of food supplies, water, timber and mining machinery, and returning with a back-load of bagged ore. Over time, Afghan camel owners and handlers not only built settlements at railheads, but also around mining camps.

Around the end of the nineteenth century, large teams of camels walked from the Oodnadatta railhead in South Australia to the Arltunga gold mine in the Northern Territory. It took the Afghan cameleers and their animals 21 days to cover the 600 kilometres, often in daily temperatures of around 40°C.

In South Australia, camels were used to collect the minerals mica and wolfram, and worked regularly with the copper ore cartage from mines in the Flinders Ranges.

In Queensland, up to 500 camels carried ore from a large copper mine in Cloncurry. The animals struggled to cope with tropical conditions in the wet season, but because the mining town was not connected to a rail link for many years, camels were vital to the mines. Camels

Will these prospectors in Western Australia, in 1895, strike it rich?

Camels drawing ploughs during construction at Port Augusta-Kalgoorlie railway line, 1912–1917.

also carried ore and coke from mines in the far west and north of Queensland.

Throughout the mining settlements in New South Wales, and around Broken Hill, camels and their handlers were an everyday scene. They were also used in the gold-bearing areas of the Murchison, Pilbara and Kimberley regions of Western Australia.

GOLD!

When the cry of 'gold' went up in 1892, a tidal wave of people rushed west!

Gold had been discovered in the red desert area the Aborigines called *goolgardie* (possibly meaning 'rock hole with mulga trees'), later named Coolgardie. Coolgardie is 600 kilometres east of Perth in Western Australia, but there was no transport to the mine area. Desperate to make their fortune, men travelled by horseback, in wagons or by foot. They carried a pick and shovel, and dishes and sieves to toss dirt and help sort surface gold from scrap. Water was too precious to use for rinsing. Food was hard to get and water almost impossible, costing the princely sum of five shillings a gallon (approximately $6 for 5 litres), if available.

The first camels to arrive in the West were from Thomas Elder's stud at Beltana, South Australia. They were shipped over and docked at the ports of Albany and Fremantle. Some were also taken to Esperance, which had no jetty, so the camels swam ashore. Coolgardie's streets were made wide so strings of camels could turn easily.

The last Cobb & Co. coach drawn by a camel team instead of horses, c. 1920.

Arrival of mail at Alice Springs.

Large numbers of camels pulled earth shovels to build dams for much needed water supplies at Coolgardie, c. 1894.

Afghan camel owners Faiz and Tagh Mahomed carted riders and provisions across the flat sandy deserts to the mine settlements or to surrounding areas in search of gold deposits. The shortage of water continued to be critical, especially during the baking hot summer months. Camels hauled heavy bore casings to help drill for underground water. And when dams were built, camels pulled the ploughs and scoops. They even carted 390,000 bags of cement for the building of the Mundaring weir.

In 1893, gold was found in nearby Kalgoorlie, but the water shortage was so severe, settlers claimed water was more precious than gold. Thousands died from the water-related disease typhoid, or from drinking contaminated water. Living conditions for the miners and their families were extremely hard and primitive. For a person to take a tin-tub bath, he or she would have had to sponge up water that had been carried from underground tanks by camel or brought from a salt-water condenser.

Families and miners relied on camels for many needs. The mailman, doctor, politician, police, priest and dentist all arrived by camel. It was a prospector though, who in 1894, discovered a reef of gold while tracking stray camels. It was 65 kilometres northwest of Coolgardie, a two-day walk for miners. He called it the 'Wealth of Nations', and it proved to be the richest mine at the time.

Camels were continually on the move. One camel owner from Western Australia says that in those days if one mine closed, 'camels were used to relocate mining equipment, and if it was sold for other purposes, to transport it there'.

Because of the waterholes situated in Fowlers Bay, South Australia, cameleers and their animals stopped in the town on their return journey from the West Australian goldfields, across the barren Nullarbor Plain to the east of the continent. Police and camel caretakers in the town first quarantined the animals. They then treated those affected with mange, a skin disease, with carbolic acid or Stockholm tar and linseed oil, before allowing them to continue.

A camel's arched back provides good support for carrying heavy loads, like the wool bales in the pictures above.

CAMEL STEW!
3 medium-sized camels
1 ton salt and 1 ton pepper
500 bushels potatoes
500 bushels carrots
3,000 sprigs parsley
2 rabbits

Method: Cut camels into bite-size pieces
(this should take about 2 months).
Cut vegetables into cubes
(another 2 months).
Place meat in pan and cover with 1,000
gallons of brown gravy.
Simmer for 4 weeks.
Shovel in salt and pepper.
When meat is tender, add vegetables.
Simmer slowly for another 4 weeks.
Serve, garnished with the parsley.

Will serve 3,800 people. If more are
expected, add the two rabbits.

A humorous outback recipe!

Strings of pack camels formed smooth tracks for bicycle riders. Their broad feet cleared loose stones and pressed pebbles and sand into the soil. But here, at Port Augusta in South Australia in 1902, a team of camels is helping to build a road by hauling a weighted roller.

LAKE CALLABONNA

Today, Lake Callabonna is a large, dry saltpan. It lies in a remote, desolate region of sand-dunes and samphire bush in the far north of South Australia.

Yet once this salt-encrusted lake contained fresh water. Fish swam in it and giant creatures came to its grassy shoreline to drink and find food.

About 50,000 years ago a long drought caused the lake to dry out. Unfortunately, a large group of the animals became bogged in the mud and died. Their bodies were preserved, and turned into fossils. It was these fossils that brought camels and their Afghan handlers to the lake.

The fossils were much sought after. They were those of a *Diprotodon*, the world's largest marsupial, about the size of a modern hippopotamus. It was a herbivore, or plant eater, so named in the Greek language because of its two large front teeth (*Di*=two, *proto*=forwards, *don*=teeth).

In 1892, the owner of Lake Callabonna and the surrounding property was describing an elephant to a local Aborigine. The Aborigine grew excited. He believed he'd seen the large bones of an elephant in the boggy lake bed.

News of this important discovery spread quickly. In 1893, the South Australian Museum sent geologist Henry Hurst and a small group, including Afghan handlers and their camels, to the area. Hurst discovered other fossils

as well, including those of a giant bird and giant wombat. He also found the fossils of a young *Diprotodon*, near its mother's pouch.

Later that year, Thomas Elder sponsored another expedition, which was led by the South Australian Museum Director, Dr Stirling and his assistant, Mr Zietz. They camped about 9 kilometres from the Callabonna homestead.

Because of the lack of feed near Stirling's camp site, the Afghans and camels that had come with him needed to camp almost 5 kilometres away. Each day, they'd journey to the homestead to collect news, mail, water and meat. The meat, however, often turned rotten within the day. When the house water supply grew alarmingly short, the Afghans walked the camels to a well, collecting firewood on the way. The trip there and back took two days.

Meanwhile, Stirling and his men excavated, month after month. They laboured in tough conditions made worse by heat, flies, gastric illness due to poor water, eye diseases and a rabbit plague.

Of the hundreds of fossilised bones they found, many were soft and powdery. Others were wet and pliable like putty. Harder, firmer fossils were carefully packed into wooden containers and then loaded onto the camels for

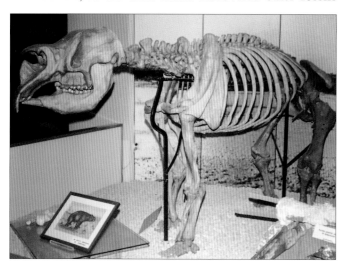

Diprotodon skeleton displayed in 1976 at the South Australian Museum in Adelaide.

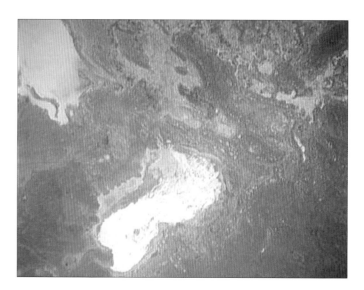

This satellite photograph clearly shows Lake Callabonna and the surrounding arid countryside.

The fossil field had little timber available for firewood. Whatever was found was stacked in a particular way for carting by camel.

transport to Adelaide. Several camels became bogged in a soggy stretch of the lake even before setting off. Fossil breakages occurred either then, or during the 320-kilometre journey to a railway station in the Flinders Ranges, where the boxes were unloaded for carting further south by rail.

Enough *Diprotodon* fossils had survived, however, for Mr Zietz to painstakingly piece together a whole skeleton and make a cast. When the cast was displayed in 1908, the world had its first view of the ancient, now extinct, marsupial.

Adventurer Robyn Davidson and her camels became lost in Central Australia. Skilled tracker Johnny Long located her by studying camel droppings. How did he know the difference between the droppings from Robyn's camels and those of feral camels? *Wild camels don't eat baked beans!*

Painstakingly unearthing fossils of a giant marsupial.

POLICE ON CAMELS

Think of police work today and you might think of high-speed car chases or emergency radio contact. A lone policeman on a camel might sound funny in comparison, but until the 1950s, that was the only law-provider for thousands of square kilometres of Australian outback.

Policemen stationed in the outback had an isolated job, living in a rugged, desert environment with only a camel for transport — a smelly animal 'which attracted every fly within a hundred miles!'

Besides needing to be tough, self-reliant and strong, the police had to be fair because they dealt with many different people: Europeans, Aborigines and Afghans; stockmen, graziers, drovers and railway workers.

The policeman stationed at Finke Police Station in the Northern Territory patrolled 220,000 square kilometres, the largest police beat in the world. The remote township of Finke was near the western edge of the Simpson Desert.

'You could see the first line of sand hills from the police house.' The beat stretched from the Queensland border to the Western Australian border, and from near Alice Springs to the South Australian border — including some stations in South Australia.

The galvanised-iron police station was attached to the police house. In the yard was a storehouse for the camel gear and police supplies, including a coffin, a storeroom for the rations, and a small cell.

The iron police house had a flywire-enclosed veranda and was hot in summer and cold in winter. There was no electricity or refrigeration. Meat and milk were kept in a makeshift cupboard, draped with wetted hessian and called a Coolgardie safe. As the moisture evaporated, so the foodstuffs inside were cooled. Butter often ran to oil.

Marree, 700 kilometres north of Adelaide, in South Australia, was once an important railhead and a busy town

Blacktracker Riley and his wife Elsie at Marree, South Australia.

Policeman Ron Brown at Adulka waterhole. The depth of the hole is the length of the stick. Although they dry up quickly in hot weather, police depended on these unmapped and irregular waterholes.

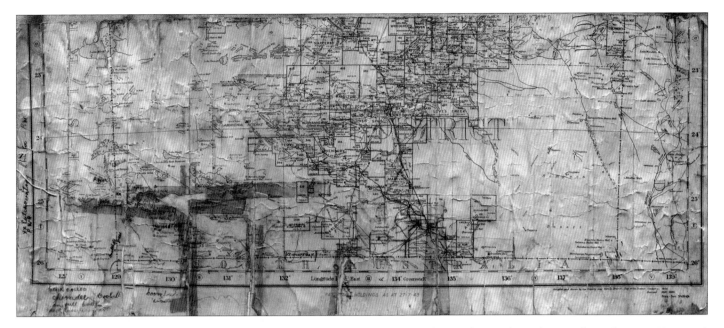

Policeman Ron Brown ('Brownie of the Finke'), mounted this portion of his map of Central Australia on hessian for endurance. He traced the Camel Patrol Route with red ink and estimated his travelling distances using a matchstick.

At the Marree Police Station in South Australia, around 1950. Cells can be seen in the background.

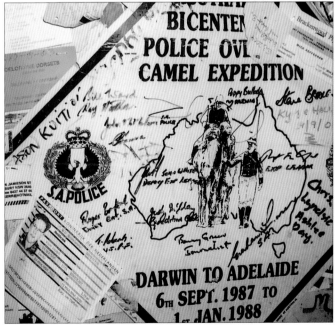

Displayed in the outback hotel at William Creek, South Australia, this sign commemorates the Bicentenary Police Overland Camel Expedition.

where cameleers loaded and unloaded goods. Cattle were droved there from southeast Queensland, down the Birdsville Track, and later, passengers arrived on the old Ghan train. The policeman stationed there patrolled a beat of 64,000 square kilometres, from Marree to Birdsville and along Coopers Creek to Innamincka. One policeman stationed there in the 1940s commented that the dust storms there were so severe that, 'when the kids woke up in the morning you could see an outline where they had been sleeping'.

Each policeman dealt with a variety of situations, large and small. He checked stock routes, settled boundary disputes, apprehended cattle thieves, arrested drunks, and searched for people lost in the outback. He often had a blacktracker, an Aboriginal skilled in the art of tracking.

Once, when a railway worker went missing in the desolate area of Lake Eyre, in northern South Australia, the policeman and tracker set off to search for him. At night, the tracker followed marks with only the glow of a hurricane lamp. They found the man alive the following morning.

Other roles of a policeman included:
- Protector of Aborigines
- Registrar of births, death and marriages
- Registrar of vehicles, firearms and dogs
- Licensing inspector
- Destroyer of dingo scalps
- Agent for the Flying Doctor
- Deliver rations of treacle, flour, tea, dress materials and blankets to old or sick Aborigines.

Often the policeman and tracker were away on patrol for weeks or months at a time. The camels would be loaded with supplies including flour, tea, sugar, salt beef, and dried fruit. Two sixteen-gallon drums of water, (total of 145 litres or 32 gallons) were strapped either side of a camel. Day after day, the men rode throughout remote areas, patrolling hundreds of kilometres of dry, rocky creek beds, flat spinifex plains or shifting sand dunes. While they were away, the policeman's wife took over his other duties.

Maps were vital on patrol. Aborigines knew the country well, but not necessarily in terms of numerical distances. If a policeman asked an Aborigine how far it was from one place to another, he or she might say, 'Supposing we leave now, travel all day till sundown today and camp, tomorrow we travel all day from daylight to sundown, and then the next day, midday, when the sun is right overhead, we get to that place then'.

Policemen therefore added landmark drawings to their maps. One policeman discovered the position of several waterholes by studying an Aboriginal dot painting. Another measured distances on his map by using a matchstick, estimating the length equalled 60 miles (96 kilometres).

Now, with modern vehicles and equipment, police no longer need to rely on the camel for outback patrols. Many former police, however, counted those years as the best in their career.

SOLDIERS ON CAMELS
'I have nothing to say, beyond that I'm very much alive

Police station and outbuildings at Finke in the Northern Territory, around 1938 or 1939.

Herding camels, preparatory to setting out on a patrol from Finke Police Station.

and that's the main thing in these parts.' Private Donald Cameron, a camelier serving in Palestine during World War I, wrote these words to his parents in Australia in 1917. At twenty he volunteered for the Anzac Camel Corps. He was one of hundreds from the Infantry and Australian Light Horse to learn to ride a camel into action. Other men of the New Zealand, English and Indian armies also volunteered. They formed the Imperial Camel Corps.

Another young camelier, Clive Arthur wrote home:

We had our first experience at handling camels yesterday. Most of the camels are covered in ticks and they gave the order to pick the ticks off. I went up to one and he snapped at me.

The Camel Corps was selected for long-range desert patrols during a period of fighting between the Allies and the Turkish Army and Serussi Arabs in 1916 — fighting which spread across the Western Desert into Palestine and Sinai. The camel was chosen because it could go without drinking for seven days in the desert, and carry heavy loads.

A desert patrol for the men in the Anzac Camel Corps meant they had to take everything necessary for seven days without support from the rest of the army. The camels carried all that was needed for battle, including rifles, bayonets, compasses, ammunition, food, blankets, and a 5-gallon drum (23 litres) of water for each camelier. Meals were often bully beef and hot tea with hard biscuits crushed up to make a kind of porridge.

To keep cool in the hot desert, cameliers cut the long sleeves and legs from their khaki shirts and trousers. Desert nights were fiercely cold and the men rugged up in their blankets, often sleeping close to their camels for warmth.

Sometimes they'd travel great distances at night, as Donald Cameron wrote:

Night marches are common occurrences in the camel corps. They are things that make you curse the war. Imagine riding along in the pitch dark from about seven o'clock at night till just about dawn the following morning, carrying on as usual the next day, snatching what rest you can, until you get to your destination, by which time you are so dog tired that you drop like a

The 4th Battalion, Anzac Section of the Imperial Camel Corps, are on the move in Abbassia, Egypt, during World War I in 1915.

stone when you have unsaddled your camel.

When the cameliers went into battle against the Turks, some men held the camels, while the rest ran or crawled to the front line. Cameliers suffered the blinding glare of the sun, swarms of flies and exhausting heat that sometimes reached 52°C. They were bombed by German aeroplanes, shelled by artillery and shot at by Turkish rifles and machine-guns. Wounded cameliers were carried from the battlefield to hospital in a cacolet, a stretcher-basket that was strapped to the side of a camel. The jolting ride often added to their pain.

The Anzac Camel Corps fought in many battles during World War I between 1916 and 1918, in places such as Magdhaba, Rafa, Gaza and Amman. Over time, many men grew to respect their camels. Some gave them names, such as Horace. Camelier Clive Arthur wrote, 'Can't say I like them better than the old horse although they don't take half the looking after.'

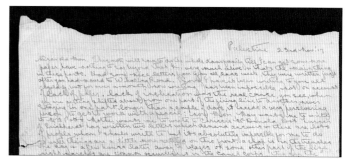

Part of Donald Cameron's letter home.

It was planned that strong camels bred in South Australia would be sent to the Middle East for the Anzac Camel Corps. But the Camel Corps was disbanded in 1918 and the cameliers were formed into the 14th and 15th Light Horse Regiments for the rest of the war.

The gravestone of a camelier.

In 1921 a memorial in the form of a bronze mounted camelier was unveiled in Victoria Gardens, London.

CAMELS IN PEOPLE'S LIVES

- In 1915, when Gladys Lynch was six years old, she and her family drove in a Model T-Ford 'up the Birdsville Track, with camels to pull us over the sand dunes and claypans, and horses to pull us through water'. The family shared johnnycakes with Afghan camel drivers, and goanna and snake caught by Aboriginal women.

- Kurt Johannsen spent part of his childhood at Deep Well, in the Northern Territory, where his father supplied water to the stock being driven to the railhead at Oodnadatta.

In 1922, the Correspondence School was started and once a month, the South Australian Education Department sent up our sets of schoolwork with the camel mail. I remember seeing four or five wool bales of possum and rabbit skins being sent away by camel, and how, the corrugated iron used for roofing was brought up by camel. The maximum length that could be carried by a camel was 10 feet [3 metres] but mostly the sheets of iron were only 8 feet [2.4 metres] long, loaded in crates. A crate on one side of the camel would be counter-balanced on the other side by another crate filled with bags of sugar, flour and other stores.

- In the 1920s, Francis Birtles spent some time with the Johannsen family. He was 'surveying places to land his aeroplane for refuelling on his forthcoming flight and waiting for some petrol to be delivered by camel'.

- From 1886 to 1913, gold was mined at Arltunga in the Northern Territory. Over a hundred miners and their families moved to the area, the largest group of Europeans to settle in central Australia at that time. Walter Smith remembered that,

the arrival of a camel train from the Wallis & Co. Store in

Around 1900, Dulcie Wing and her family travelled by camel from South Australia, across the Nullarbor Plain, to live in Western Australia.

Oodnadatta was a weekly event. Wine was carried in kegs, beer by the case and the staple rations were delivered to outback mining camps along with medical supplies like ointments, Condy's crystals and turps that stung like blazes, used as a common salve for scratches and blisters.

- Mrs E. Morton remembered:

The camel teams brought supplies yearly from the railhead to Birdsville. A usual order would be: 1 ton flour, quarter of a ton salt, 12 cases honey, half a ton sugar, 12 cases jam with sauces, pickles and other items as required — not forgetting half a ton of horseshoes, nails and hobble chains. Our billiard table was safely carried by one camel about 200 miles [320km] distance. Our children had few toys, but imagination and inventiveness made up for a lot. Empty bottles tied by string and dragged along served to represent a laden camel team, accompanied by "hushda" (sit down) and "wha-wha" (get up).

- In 1895, N.E. Phillipson, an authority on camels, commented, 'There is no reason why a lady should not ride a camel, if she is fond of this kind of exercise, and likes to be high up in the world'.

In 1922, under the guidance of an Aboriginal tracker, 11 year-old Duncan Stott rode 1,200 kilometres from Alice Springs to Port Augusta. There he took a train to begin boarding school in Adelaide.

PEST OR RESOURCE?

• Between 1840 and 1907, over 10,000 camels were imported to Australia from North Africa and Asia.

• In 2004, there are between 500,000 and 700,000 feral camels in Australia.

• The Australian camel has no natural predators or other population controls.

• It thrives on Australian vegetation.

• Its soft footpads cause far less environmental damage than the hard hoofs of feral goats and donkeys.

Wildlife scientist Sam and camel businessman Chris might discuss whether camels are a pest or resource like this:

Sam: Wild camels are infesting the continent. Their numbers could *double* every eight years. Something must be done.

Chris: Camels have always thrived in Australia.

Sam: They're fouling water supplies, damaging fences, swarming into outback properties and National Parks. They're on outback roads. Drivers are at risk.

Chris: Camels are more numerous now in those areas, but we're creating a strong industry here and overseas.

Sam: We must do major culls. Aerial culling with trained operators. We've got to cut down large numbers.

Chris: We don't want to see random culling. The camel industry's opinions need to be heard.

Sam: Camel populations are increasing and often in very remote areas, where no vehicle can get through. We have to do aerial culls.

Chris: Presently it costs about $40 for each camel culled that way. We're developing a livestock export, providing camels for breeding, racing, dairying and meat. Our business means camels don't need to be culled in such huge numbers. We want everyone to benefit.

Sam: Yes, but too few are being captured and exported. Camel numbers are growing faster than their removal. It's great if businesses can make money while the camel population is being reduced, but we've got to manage the population better.

Chris: So, let's work on ways to increase the demand for camels and camel meat.

Sam: Well, then, maybe we can rethink the culling program. But we need to be active right now.

In 2003, six dromedaries were flown to Seoul in Korea, to star in the opera *Aida* by Verdi. Before they left, their owner played them the music. She was sure they swung their tails in time!

The steady increase in Australia's camel population is the cause of much debate and decision making. Here, a helicopter tracks a herd of feral camels in the outback (left), while another (right) musters for export.

For over 70 years, camels were the road trains of the outback. Their well-worn tracks spider-webbed across vast, dry lands. People and industries in those places could not have survived without them. Then in the 1920s and 30s, cars and trucks came to the deserts and camels were no longer needed. Many were released into the wild.

WILD HERDS

Unrestricted, the camels formed herds and continued to breed. With no natural predators, and thriving on their diet of Australian shrubs and trees, the camel numbers grew alarmingly until there were hundreds of thousands of them!

Cries erupted from many involved on the land: The camels are running wild! Trampling stock fences, allowing cattle to escape, spreading weeds and damaging the environment! They must be destroyed or culled!

Something had to be done, but what? Shooting was costly. Tourists wanted to experience camel rides and treks, but tourist farms needed only a handful of camels, and each of those lived a long life. Was there another solution?

Because Australia has the largest disease-free camel population in the world, the strongest suggestion from those involved in the camel industry was to export these fine camels to other countries. In countries where camel breeding and meat consumption was traditional, healthy animals would be welcomed. Australia's camels could be used to improve these countries' own camel stock or used for meat or in some instances set up for dairying. Exporting live camels would mean a reduction in the Australian camel population while the sale of camels would fetch an income.

At first some shipping companies refused to carry the animals. Others charged exorbitant fees. Now Australia exports camels for breeding, meat, racing and dairying. They're shipped out hundreds at a time, or flown in jumbo jets to places including South East Asia, China, Hong Kong, Canada, Europe, the United States of America and the Middle East.

But are camel products sold within Australia?

MEAT

Camel meat was first obtained from animals slaughtered in an abattoir in Alice Springs in the Northern Territory in 1988. The meat is high in body-building protein and iron and its taste and texture is thought to be midway between beef and lamb. Because the camel's fat is concentrated in its hump, the meat is very trim. A lean beef steak has 12 grams of fat, whereas a lean camel steak has 1.8 grams.

Camels are now trucked to an abattoir at Strathalbyn, in South Australia. There the meat is processed for sales to supermarkets, restaurants and tourist locations throughout Australia. Camel meat can be cooked in all ways except grilling, because with so little fat, the meat becomes tough. However, it's great smoked or in sausages and burgers!

In a muster, camel handlers take as much care as possible to keep the animals calm. Any stress tends to darken the camels' meat and give it an unpleasant taste. Bulls cannot be butchered while they are rutting either, because the concentration of their body odour spoils the meat.

Camel meat can be cooked in a variety of ways. It has the approval of the National Heart Foundation.

Many camel herds criss-cross Aboriginal lands, and today several Aboriginal communities have created businesses to capture, yard and sell camels for export, meat and other products.

MILK

One day you may slurp on a camel-milk smoothie or a milkshake, or even lick a camel-milk ice-cream! For centuries camel milk has not only been the staple drink for desert-living nomads, it is also said to have mystical properties.

Some say it's similar in taste to cow's milk, but with a different aftertaste. Others comment on its sweetness. It is white, full of calcium and has health properties beneficial to diabetics, asthmatics, people with lactose intolerance and those suffering with skin problems.

It takes a lot of time to milk camels. The animals often kick without warning and so the milker has to be wary. The camel has a four-teat udder, the same as a cow's, but much smaller. Milking machines speed up the process by allowing more camels to be milked at the same time.

There is potential for a camel dairy industry in Australia. Some camel owners are considering it. Others are already working towards it as part of their business. The milk could be exported as well as used as a tourist attraction.

LEATHER

Camel skin makes great leather. It has five times the pulling strength of cattle hide, is flexible, and can be tanned like the skin of any other animal in the bovine, or ox-like, family. Traditional tanning of the hide uses tannins from trees and grasses, but modern methods use 'chrome' or chemical tanning. The hide is split in half so the hump section can be flattened. This enables tanning to be carried out in commercially available machines.

In Australia, camel leather comes from the hide after the camel has been used for meat. It can be tanned with the fur on or off, and the tanning recipes used are based on what the leather will be used for. For example, if the leather chosen for boots is too soft, it won't hold its shape.

Camel leather has many uses, both practical and fashionable. Hats, jackets, sporting goods, riding boots and wallets are all available. But so too are fashion items like shoes and clothing. It's an unusual, stippled leather, often

Beautiful, strong, useful and fashionable. These are some of the products made from camel leather.

still marked with scratches from the feral animal's desert wanderings. With new overseas markets developing, it's likely Australian camel outfits and belts will be worn on the catwalks of high fashion houses in Europe.

WOOL

Camels grow wool for warmth. In winter the Bactrian, or two-humped camel, faces freezing conditions in the Mongolian Gobi Desert in China, so it develops a thick mass of wool to keep warm. Spun into yarn, the soft, strong fibre, similar to cashmere, is used to make many goods including rope, mats, clothing and blankets.

Winters in the desert regions of Australia are bitterly cold, but mostly dry. The dromedary, the one-humped camel, grows a winter coat, but not with the abundance of the Bactrian's. Normally a dromedary has thicker wool, approximately 4 –12 centimetres long, on its shoulder, hump and neck areas, but it sheds its all-over winter coat when it gets hot. It moults according to season. Sometimes it rubs against fences, trees and bushes to help rid itself of the wool. The average wool clip of males weighs 3 kilograms and 2 kilograms for females. It's a small amount compared to the Bactrian, whose moult weight is 12–15 kilograms for males and 6–8 kilograms for

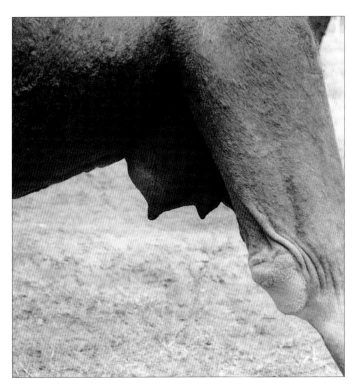

A camel's teat is similar to a cow's, but smaller.

It's believed that camels have good memories and always remember if they've been badly treated!

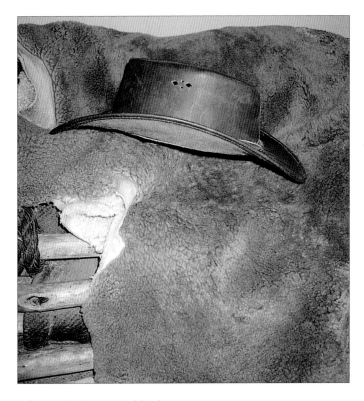

A hat made from camel leather.

Camel wool is often combined with other fibres, like sheep wool or silk. Because of the beauty of the colour, camel-wool garments are often left their natural camel colour, or dyed grey or a darker brown.

females. Wool suppliers are faced with a time-consuming task of separating the long hair from the wool that grows in the three main areas of the camel.

Presently the number of those collecting dromedary wool is not enough to create a large industry in Australia, however, smaller businesses do exist. They make garments such as hats or scarves to sell to shops or tourists.

Camel wool is called a 'luxury fibre' in the fashion world and is used to make fine suits, coats and quality knitwear. Rarer still is the white wool from albino camels. Several have been born in Australia and their wool is thought to be worth about $1,000 per kilogram.

Fine camel hairs are also used to make artists' brushes.

COSMETICS

Ever thought of lathering yourself with camel soap? Soaps, creams and cosmetics can all be made from camel oil. The oil is obtained by rendering down, or boiling, the pure fat in the camel hump. Next to the whale, camel fat is the purist of all animal fats, and contains no blood vessels to discolour or spoil the products.

In 1891, newly-wed Amelia Gillen had her precious piano carted from South Australia to her new home in Alice Springs — on the back of a camel!

GOOD GARDENERS

A THORNY PROBLEM?

Weeds are a perennial problem for farmers. However, camels like particular weeds. In certain rural areas of Queensland two of the woody, problem weeds are *parkinsonia* and *prickly acacia*. The government has spent large amounts of money trying to eradicate them by plowing or ripping, or by the use of herbicides or insects as biological agents.

Could camels help solve a thorny problem? Both *parkinsonia* and *prickly acacia* have sharp spines or thorns. However, the roof of a camel's mouth is extraordinarily tough and one Queensland camel handler believes the longer, harder and sharper the thorn is, the more the camels seem to like it!

So, in the late 1990s, Central Australian camel producers sold thousands of feral camels to Queensland pastoralists who put them on rural properties. There the camels could munch to their hearts' content. This has produced good results.

Pastoralists have also found running both cattle *and* camels (co-grazing) on their properties an advantage. Neither animal out-eats the other's food source, and camels eat the problem weeds, along with shrubs and trees — rather like garbage-disposal units! Apart from making the camels strong and healthy, it also makes pasture available for the natural grasses that cattle love.

Far away, in the lush, green pastures and mild climate of the Sapphire Coast in New South Wales, three other camels provide eco-friendly, weed-control services. Lawrence, Tut Tut and Zut Zut are steadily changing the appearance of a farming property. They are eating their way through paddocks of purple Patterson's curse (Salvation Jane), rambling blackberry, spiky

Camels eat thorny *mesquite* and *prickly acacia*. Buffel grass (right) came from seeds in cameleers' saddles.

Scotch thistle, rosa species (wild rose) and sharp pointed African boxthorn. The camels' owners believe camels provide a sensible long-term solution to the weed problem. Poisons are too expensive and harm the land. There has been much interest in the project from other farmers.

In Central Australia, it's believed that buffel grass (*Cenchrus ciliaris*) germinated from seeds brought over in the late 1800s by the Afghan cameleers. The grass had been used as padding in their camel saddles. Over time, seeds dropped, and enough took root in the ground for the robust plant to make a home for itself.

During wet seasons, the grass spreads freely. Opinions now vary as to whether it's a blessing or a curse. Although still valued as a purpose-planted fodder for cattle, and a useful plant for combating enormous dust storms, in its dry state it's a severe fire hazard, and burns hotter than natural grass.

Maybe the humped weed-eaters are playing a part in the eradication of these problem weeds.

Camels and cattle co-grazing on a property.

Four camels munching happily on boxthorn.

HAVE YOU EVER RIDDEN A CAMEL?

Camel rides have been available for many years at fairs, festivals or picnic days. Nowadays over 50 camel farms in Australia offer many other camel experiences, ranging from yard rides and short treks to safaris lasting days, weeks or months. There are speciality rides to view breathtaking sunsets or sunrises, or stately rides to outback dinners. Camels can also be hitched to a wagon and led along bush tracks, like station trails, or beside the old Ghan railway.

Other camel safaris are designed to give the participants a sense of what it was like to be an authentic explorer in Australia. Their camels carry food supplies, and water for drinking and cooking, but none for washing. Before setting off, participants are taught how to catch a camel, hobble it, pick prickles from its fur, load it, and ride it. Then, by keeping clear of the well-known tracks, and using only a map and compass, skilled handlers guide the trekkers through a variety of country and along pioneer trails. The safari members learn about desert ecology, and often encounter signs of ancient Aboriginal life or historical European settlement.

Camels and Afghan cameleers were an essential part of early outback life. Nowadays, as people learn more about camels, they often become curious about the lives of the Afghans, and the explorers and pioneers of Australia. That interest has inspired many individuals and groups to re-enact particular outback crossings or events: desert treks of the past.

• In 1977, one couple retraced the 1858 expedition of explorer John McDouall Stuart. They travelled across sand-dunes and saltbush in the far north of South Australia, country which Stuart described as some of the most dismal he'd ever seen.

• In 1987, a group of police travelled from Darwin to Adelaide to celebrate the Australian Bicentenary Police Overland Camel Expedition.

• During the Centenary of Federation in 2001, a camel trek followed the original route taken by explorers Burke

Tourists enjoy a leisurely camel ride at sunset on Cable Beach in Broome, Western Australia.

A camel having a well-earned rest between rides on a tourist farm in Central Australia.

Camel shadows on a safari ride.

Two girls settle themselves for a ride on a camel farm in Central Australia.

and Wills. Four men with their camels and a horse left Melbourne, Victoria, and headed to the Gulf of Carpentaria in the continent's north.

• In the Year of the Outback, 2002, The Last Camel Train involved a 540-kilometre trek. Dozens of camels and their handlers travelled from the old railhead at Oodnadatta in South Australia to the Telegraph Station at Alice Springs in the Northern Territory. Led by some of the descendants of the original camel drivers, they followed the old Ghan railway. The camels were loaded with 'tuckerboxes' and mail as in the early days. The trek honoured the Afghans, and also celebrated the part European cameleers and Aborigines played in opening up the inland.

Others who've made particular treks have written books about their experiences or put their writings on websites.

Camels highlight the adventure and history of the Australian outback. Today, there are camel races, camel products for sale and camel logos designed on wine glasses, menus and the transcontinental train, the Ghan.

Camel rides are popular everywhere! Here, children enjoy a ride at Brighton Beach in South Australia.

SADDLE UP!

It's time for a camel race! Camels naturally walk or pace, but when put to the gallop, they can pound at speeds of 30–50 kilometres per hour. In overseas desert countries camel racing has long been a tradition. In Australia it began in the 1900s as a fun activity at picnics or fairs. Now there are over fifteen camel races held regularly around the country — in outback and coastal venues, with both men and women jockeys.

Camel racing began in earnest when two Northern Territorians challenged each other as to whose camel was faster. Thus, the International Camel Cup was born. The first race was held in 1971 on the dry bed of the Todd River in Alice Springs in the Northern Territory. The prize money was donated to charity, and still is, while the race continues in a different venue, as a popular annual tourist event.

Spectators enjoy the frenzied commotion as jockeys, trainers and officials try to get the camels to sit before starting. Then, on the signal, it's a flurry of dust and confusion as some animals take off in full-stride, others refuse to budge and still others turn around and pelt off in the opposite direction! In some races, camels now begin in a standing position with a starting barrier.

Nowadays, there's also a professional side to camel racing, with big prize money. Those involved in the industry discuss how and where to run the races. Coastal areas attract large crowds and race distances are shorter, but the race surface is grass, whereas camels that run in remote areas, like at the Boulia Desert Sands race in Queensland, can race on sand. However, while those races reflect the outback setting, the race distances are longer, Arabian style.

Camels ridden in Middle East and Arabian countries have longer legs and smaller humps, and have been trained over centuries to run distances of up to 10 kilometres. Top, trained camels have been clocked at over 72 kilometres per hour.

The majority of camels originally imported to Australia were work animals that have bred the typical Australian camel of today. It's sturdy, well-built and better at racing shorter distances. Consequently, camels that first ran in long-distance races overseas didn't perform very well, although they were still considered favourable as breeding animals.

Wealthy overseas sheiks own huge camel studs with prize breeding camels valued at anything up to 10 million American dollars. They buy Australian camels for 'sport and stock supply'. One sheik chose 33 from a muster of 1000 and flew them home by private jet.

While camel racing in Australia may never rival horse racing, it is gaining popularity and much research is being done to produce better racing animals.

Can camels swim? Apparently they can!

It's messy, confused and unpredictable. It's the start of a camel race!

Camels racing at the popular Camel Cup, held annually in Alice Springs in the Northern Territory.

abattoir	place where animals are slaughtered for food
acacia	a tree or shrub, found particularly in Australia
aerial	inhabiting or spending time in the air
alluvial gold	gold found in soil, mud or sand in streams
back-load	a load to carry on a return journey
Bactrian	a two-humped camel
bayonet	a stabbing instrument; fitted to a rifle
billycan	a lidded metal container for boiling water
bladder	any inflatable bag
bluebush	a native shrub with high salt content
boundary rider	a station hand who tends to fences and stock
bullocky	the driver of a bullock team
cairn	a heap of stones set up as a landmark
camelier	World War I soldier who rode camels into action
cashmere	fine, downy hair of Kashmir goats of India
chaff	straw cut small for fodder or animal food
chapattis	flat, round Indian bread made without yeast
coke	product left after coal is heated in a closed chamber
condenser	an apparatus to reduce a gas or vapour to liquid
corrugated iron	metal for building, formed into grooves
crossbreed	to produce a new species, using two breeds or varieties
cull	to kill animals in order to control numbers
cummerbund	a shawl or sash worn as a belt
dingo	the Australian wild dog
domestic animal	living with humans; tame
draught animal	an animal used to pull a load
dromedary	a one-humped camel
endangered	threatened with becoming extinct
eucalypt	any tree belonging to the eucalyptus family
evaporation	the giving off of moisture
excavate	to make a hole as by digging, to remove material
exportation	sending goods out of the country, usually for trade
feral	wild, or existing in a state of nature
flanks	the side of an animal between the ribs and hips
flannel	a warm, soft fabric
galvanised iron	zinc coated iron; prevents rust
geologist	a scientist who deals with the rocks of the earth
gibber plains	a flat area made up of stones or boulders
goanna	a large Australian lizard
grazier	owner of a rural sheep or cattle property
habitat	the place where an animal or plant naturally lives
halter	a rope or strap for leading or fastening animals
hawker	someone who travels from place to place selling goods
herbicide	a chemical that kills plants or hinders their growth
hessian	strong fabric made from jute
hobble	to fasten together the legs to stop free movement
importation	the bringing in of goods from another country
insulator	material that is a non-conductor of electricity, heat or sound

johnnycake	a small flat damper of flour, cooked in embers of a campfire or in a camp oven
khaki	a dull green with a yellowish or brownish tinge
latitude	the angular distance north or south from the equator of a point on the earth's surface
longitude	the angular distance east or west on the earth's surface, measured along the equator
mallee	eucalyptus with branching stems from underground wood tuber
mange	a skin disease causing hair loss and scabby sores
membrane	a thin, movable sheet or tissue
mica	pearl-like mineral that splits easily
migrate	to go from one place or country to live in another
mosque	a Muslim temple or place of worship
moult	to cast, or shed feathers or skin
nomads	people who travel from place to place
outback	remote, sparsely inhabited land
pastoralist	owner of property for grazing stock
pigweed	a succulent or juicy plant
plague	a severe number of insects or rodents
predator	a creature that preys on others for food
prospector	someone who searches for minerals
railhead	the farthest point to which a railway has been laid
rawhide	untreated animal skin or hide
ringbark	to cut around part of a tree to kill it
rum	an alcohol spirit from a sugarcane product
saltbush	a drought-resistant bush
samphire bush	a succulent herb
sand dune	a hill or ridge of sand formed by the wind
spinifex	spiny-leaved, tussock-forming grasses
stipple	to cover an area with dots or spots
succulent	full of juice
survey	to decide on form, boundaries, position and extent of the earth's surface by measurement
tarpaulin	protective covering of canvas or other material made waterproof with tar, paint or wax
tuckerbox	any box used to hold food
turban	form of headdress, worn mainly by Muslim men; a long piece of material wound round the head
water bore	a deep hole, bored into underground water supply
wolfram	a mineral of heavy dark crystals

ACKNOWLEDGEMENTS

I am deeply grateful to three wonderful *camel men*: Peter Seidel, Chief Executive Officer of the Central Australian Camel Industry Association; Noel Fullerton, well-known and experienced camel owner/handler and founder of the Alice Springs Camel Cup race; and Paddy McHugh, Chairman of the Queensland Camel Industry Association, Managing Director of Australian Camel Farm and founder of the Boulia Desert Sands Camel Races. All willingly gave their time and expertise to assist with information, photographs and reviewing the manuscript.

Special thanks too to Margaret and Max Hamilton, and others who helped the project: namely Michelle Fullerton, Allan Homes, John Nightingale (Curator of Botany, Alice Springs Desert Park), Noel McKay (Coolgardie Camel Farm), Neville Pledge (Honorary Researcher, Curator of Fossils), Pat Jackson and Kym Muller (NT Archives Service), Tina Dunemann (Port Augusta Public Library), Jill Evans (S.A. Museum Archives Service), South Australian Maritime Museum, Maggy Ragless, Michael Charteris, Tabitha Zarins, Grace Reid, David Whitelaw, Geoff Sainty, John Hare, Alison Bird, Ron Blum, Mel Davies, Bob Kessing, the family of Duncan Stott, Audrey Robson, Elizabeth Hutchins, Dulcie King, Sid Boucher and Jon Grant. *For those I've inadvertently omitted to mention, my sincere apologies and thanks.*

PHOTOGRAPHIC CREDITS

KEY: top (t), bottom (b), left (l), right (r)
Alison Bird, (© Bruce Falconer, T/A Broome Photography), **p 57**, endpapers; Allan Homes, **p 25** (t), **p 26** (t/r), **p 29** (m), **p 46** (l) **p 47** (l); Australian National Library, **p 27** (b) (neg. NL21797 M.H Robinson. Ellison Collection) **p 28** (r) (A 52, m32414 M. Jean Chaylet Collection); Australian War Memorial, **p 49** (neg.no. H02693), **p 50** (t) (PR88/094); Central Australian Tourist Information Association, **p 59** (r) © Jim Cowie; Courtesy Battye Library, **p 40** (LISWA Catalogue, Roy Millar Collection, no. 008948D 4007B/20); Courtesy of Earth Sciences and Image Analysis Laboratory, NASA Johnson Space Centre, **p 44** (r) Image STS008-49-1760. JPG website: http://eol.jsc.nasa.gov; Dulcie Wing, **p 51** (l); family of Duncan Stott, **p 41** (b), **p 51** (r); Geoff Sainty, **p 56** (t), (m); Grace Reid, **p 38** (b/l), **p 41** (m) (Partridge Collection, Old Timers' Museum, NT); Janeen Brian (author), imprint page, **p 11** (b), **p 13**, **p 18** (t), (b/l), (b/r), **p 19** (t) (t/r), **p 21** (m) (b/l) (b/r), **p 25** ((b/r), **p 30** (l) (m) (r), **p 34** (m), **p 35** (b), **p 39** (t/r) (m), (b), **p 47** (b/r) **p 55** (t/l) (b), **p 58** (t) (b/l) (b/r), **p 59** (l) back cover (t/l) (b); John Hare, **p 8** (r) (Wild Camel Protection Foundation,

School Farm, Benedene, Kent TN17 4EU); John Nightingale, **p 56**, (t/r); Lutheran Archives, **p 38** (b/r); Maggy Ragless, Hans Mincham & Vern McIntosh Collection, **p 23** (t/l), **p 25** (b/l), **p 26** (t/l), **p 28** (b/l), **p 29** (t), **p 43** (t) (m), **p 44** (l); Matt Bryksy, **p 9** (t) (b); Michael Charteris, **p 50** (l) (b/r); Michelle Smail, **p 37**; National Railway Museum, Port Adelaide, **p 36** (D. Colquhoun Collection); Noel Fullerton, **p 11** (m), **p 15** (t/l) (t/r) (m), **p 19** (b), **p 20**, **p 21** (t), **p 23** (t/r) (b), **p 24**, **p 25** (m), **p 26** (b/l) (b/r), **p 29** (b), **p 34** (t) (b), **p 39** (t/l), **p 41** (t), **p 58** (m); Northern Territory Archives Service, **p 46** (r) (Brown, Ron A NTRS 1641, Item 2. Ron Brown at Adulka waterhole), **p 47** (t) (m) (NTRS 855 Item 1 Centralian Camel Patrol Map, 1945–52), **p 48** (l) (NTRS 1641/P1 Item 17 Finke Police Station and outbuildings, c 1938/9), **p 48** (r) (Item 8 herding camels preparatory to patrol — Finke NT); Paddy McHugh, **p 15** (b), **p 52** (l) (r); Peter Seidel, title page, introduction, **p 10**, **p 12** (t) (m) (b), **p 14**, **p 16** map, (t) (b), **p 17** (t) (m) (b/l) (b/r), **p 31** (b/l), **p 53**, **p 54**, **p 55** (t/r), **p 56** (b/l) back cover (t/r); Photograph courtesy of the State Library of South Australia, **p 32**, **p 42**, back cover (b/r); Port Augusta Public Library (Local History Collection), **p 22**; Ron Blum Collection, **p 43** (b); S. Kidman and Co., **p 38** (t); South Australian Museum Photographic Library, **p 45** (t) (b); Tabitha Zarins, **p 56** (b/r) *All effort has been made to source references and acknowledge accurately.*

BIBLIOGRAPHY

Anderson, R. J. *Solid town: The History of Port Augusta.* Anderson, Port Augusta, SA, 1988

Barker, H. M. *Camels and the Outback.* Pitman, Melbourne, 1964

Cigler, Michael. *The Afghans in Australia.* AE Press, Melbourne, 1986

Cloudsey-Thompson, John. *Camels.* Wayland, East Sussex, 1980

Colwell, Max and David. *Australia's Timeless Land.* Max Colwell, Joslin, SA, 1984

Earle, Olive L. *Camels and Llamas.* George J. McLeod Ltd, Toronto, 1961

Johannsen, Kurt G. *The Son of the Red Centre.* K. G. Johannsen, Morphettville, SA, 1992

Langley, George F and Edmee M. *Sand, Sweat and Camels.* Rigby, Adelaide, 1976

Mincham, Hans. *The Story of the Flinders Ranges.* Rigby, Adelaide, 1964

Ragless, Margaret E. *Dust Storms in China Teacups.* Investigator Press, Hawthorndene, SA, 1988

Rajkowski, Pamela. *In the Tracks of the Camelmen.* Angus & Robertson, Sydney, 1987

Smith, Penny. *A Ton of Spirit.* Allen & Unwin, Sydney, 1990

Stevens, Christine. *Tin Mosques and Ghan Towns.* Oxford University Press, Melbourne, 1989